Du

Start Building
Your Vocabulary

John Flow

Australia Canada   ed Kingdom United St

Start Building Your Vocabulary
John Flower

Publsiher/Global ELT: *Christopher Wenger*
ExecutiveMarketing Manager/Global ELT/ESL: *Amy Mabley*

Printed in Croatia by Zrinski
3 4 5 6 7 8 9 10   06

For more information contact Heinle, 25 Thomson Place, Boston, MA 02210 USA,
or you can visit our Internet site at http://www.heinle.com

ISBN 1-899396-05-5

The Author
John Flower is a teacher at Eurocentre, Bournemouth where he worked for many years. He has
long experience of teaching students at all levels. He is author of the Build Your Vocabulary
series, First Certificate Organiser, and Phrasal Verb Organiser.

Acknowledgements
Cover design by Anna Macleod
Illustrations by James Slate and Anna Macleod

Contents

Chapter One

Start Building Your Vocabulary

1. **Words are the most important things you can learn.**

   English has the largest vocabulary in the world. Grammar is important, but vocabulary is much more important.

2. **There is not enough time in class to learn a lot of words.**

   Your teacher has many different things to do in class. If you want to improve, you must learn words on your own, at home, on the bus, watching television – everywhere!

3. **Keep a vocabulary notebook.**

   Write down the new words and phrases you learn. Organise your vocabulary notebook so that you can look things up again.

4. **This chapter is important.**

   Study this chapter first. The ideas here will help you learn better.

1.1 How to use this book

1. Before you start the units, study the whole of this chapter first.

2. When you have finished Chapter 1, choose from each chapter. For example, do 2.1, then 3.1, then 4.1 - this will be more interesting.

3. To help you learn vocabulary, you will need two other books:
    - a good dictionary
    - a vocabulary notebook

4. Use your vocabulary notebook every day to write in words and expressions which you think are important.

1.2 Some important words

The words on the left are used at the beginning of this book. Match them with the phrases on the right. Write your answers in the box below.

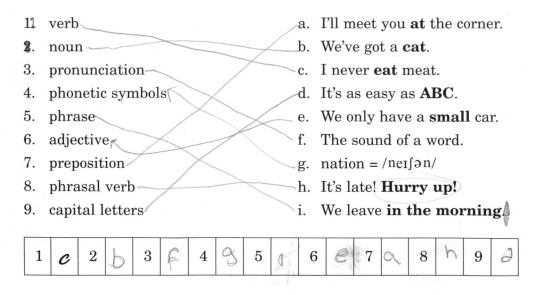

1. verb
2. noun
3. pronunciation
4. phonetic symbols
5. phrase
6. adjective
7. preposition
8. phrasal verb
9. capital letters

a. I'll meet you **at** the corner.
b. We've got a **cat**.
c. I never **eat** meat.
d. It's as easy as **ABC**.
e. We only have a **small** car.
f. The sound of a word.
g. nation = /neɪʃən/
h. It's late! **Hurry up!**
i. We leave **in the morning**.

1	c	2	b	3	f	4	g	5	i	6	e	7	a	8	h	9	d

1.3 Find the right word

Find these words in your dictionary. Which two can you use to talk about going on a bus?

answer   catch   example   fare   vowel

1.4 Word partnerships

When you see a word in a dictionary, look at the examples. Which other words are often used with it?

Match a verb on the left with a noun on the right. Use each word once only. Write the words together like the example:

1. speak — a bath
2. do — a bike
3. have — a bus
4. make — English
5. play — TV
6. ride — your homework
7. catch — a mistake
8. watch — golf

speak English . . . . . .
. . do a mistake . . . . .
. . have a bath . . . . .
. . make a bath . .
. . play golf . . . . . .
. . ride a bike . . .
. . catch a bus .
. . watch TV . . . . .

Now use some of the answers to complete these sentences:

9. You can . . catch . . (a bus) from the stop outside the station.

10. Does Eva . . . . ? > She only knows a few words.

11. What's your favourite sport? > I often . . . . but I prefer football.

12. Do you . . . . very much? > Not really. Most of the programmes are so stupid!

1.5 Word families

When you find a word in a dictionary, see if you can make other words from it, for example:

information > inform   use > useful > useless

Change each word at the end to complete the sentence.

1. I like it here. Everybody's so . . . . . *friendly* . . . . . (FRIEND)
2. If the sea is too cold, you can use the . . . swim . . pool. (SWIM)
3. Don't walk on the road! It's very . . . danger . . . . ! (DANGER)
4. On her wall she has a copy of a . . . paint . . . . . by Dali. (PAINT)
5. Have you got any . . inform . . about your English classes? (INFORM)
6. I don't want to go out. It's so cold and . . . wind . . . . . . ! (WIND)

1.6 Pronunciation

A dictionary uses symbols - phonetic symbols - to show you how to say a word. If you learn these symbols, you will also know a word's pronunciation.

In this exercise there are three ways of saying the letter 'o'. Put each word in the correct group.

brother	close	come	copy	front	go
home	hot	job	long	love	money
most	often	one	open	show	stop

1. /ʌ/   2. /ɒ/   3. /əʊ/

one ....   hot ....   go ....

....

....

....

....

1.7 Words in sentences

When you find a new word that you want to put in a vocabulary list, it is a good idea to write a sentence using the word. This will help you understand and remember the word.

Put these words in the right place. Add any other helpful information - for example, the translation.

artist	delicious	department store	give up	hurry
of course	out of order	recommend	shampoo	terrible

1. *hurry* .... = **go quickly**

   I must . *hurry* . . . or I'll be late for work.

2. ....*terrible*.... = **good to eat**

   Can I have some more, please. This is . *delicious*

3. *artist* .... = **somebody who paints pictures**

   Salvador Dali is Helen's favourite . . *artist* . .

4. *of course* .. = **Certainly/Yes**

   Can I have something to drink? - *of . . . Course* you can.

5. *out of order* .... = **stop**

   You must *out of o* ... smoking! You know it's bad for you!

6. *department store* ...= **big shop selling many different things**

   You can buy almost anything you want in this *department store*

7. ....*terrible*.... = **very bad**

   The weather is *terrible*! It's very cold and wet.

8. *give up* ... = **not working**

   I can't use the phone. It's *give up* d

9. *recommend* . = **tell someone that something is good**

   I don't know any good restaurants. Can you *recommend* one?

10. *shampoo* . = **a liquid for washing your hair**

    This new *shampoo* washes my hair much better.

1.8 Words from texts

When you read a text in English, look at it again and see what useful words and phrases you can find. Don't look for single words but notice the way in which words go together.

Read the following story. Underline any vocabulary you think is useful.

A Traveller's Story

I hate flying. It's the worst way to travel. First of all, your plane leaves at 10 o'clock in the morning. Fine. But you have to be there at 8. You live 50 miles from the airport. So, you leave home at 6. That means getting up at 5. Crazy!

You don't want to be late, so you take a taxi. The trains are terrible, but the traffic is awful! You sit in a traffic jam for 45 minutes. Are you going to miss your plane?

No. You arrive just in time. But now you stand in a queue at the check-in for another half an hour. In front of you is a noisy family of eight and an elderly couple who can't find their passports. Then you stand in another queue at passport control for 15 minutes. You are not happy!

Finally, you go through passport control. You have exactly 8 minutes to buy something from the duty-free shop before it's time to board the plane. Then you have a long journey in front of you. The seats are very small. The person sitting next to you is very fat. He wants to tell you his life story . . . .

That's what normally happens. But yesterday it was different. Yesterday the person sitting next to me on the plane was a tall thin man with long black hair and dark glasses. He didn't say a word to me for over an hour. When the flight attendant brought drinks, he refused. When she brought lunch, he refused again.

Suddenly, the man stood up. He took something out of his travel bag. It was a gun. People started to scream. The flight attendant came over to us.

"Can I help you, sir?" she asked.

"Take me to Havana – or I'll blow the plane up!"

The flight attendant smiled.

"Please sit down, sir. Havana's where we're going. Now, what would you like to drink?"

Exercise

Now look at these phrases from the text. Write the missing words.

1. Noun + Noun

traffic jam   . . . . . . control   . . . . . . attendant   . . . . . . bag

2. Verb + Noun

. . . . . . home   . . . . . . a taxi   . . . . . . your plane   . . . . . . the plane

3. Verb + Preposition + Noun

You stand . . . . a queue.

You go . . . . passport control.

You buy something . . . . the duty-free shop.

4. Time Expressions

Your plane leaves . . . . 10 o'clock . . . . the morning.

You sit in a traffic jam . . . . 45 minutes.

5. Common Adjectives

A tall thin . . . . with long black . . . . and dark

. . . .

6. Phrasal Verbs

You leave home at 6. That means getting . . . . at 5!

Suddenly, the man stood . . . .

"Take me to Havana or I'll blow the plane . . . . !"

7. Useful Expressions

" . . . . I help you?"

"Please sit . . . ."

"What would you . . . . to drink?"

8. Can you find some more useful words and expressions? Write them here:

. . . .

. . . .

. . . .

1.9 Words from pictures

Using pictures can help you remember words. Some exercises in this book use pictures, but you can make your own picture dictionary. Cut pictures out of magazines or draw them yourself. Don't worry if you can't draw very well.

Here are 12 phrases. Write them below the correct picture:

short and fat   tall and thin   thin and bald   old and poor
young and happy   wet and windy   nice and sunny   tired and dirty
tired and sleepy   rich and famous   hot and angry   nice and tasty

1. tired and dirty.   2. tin and bald.   3. tired and sleepy

4. old and poor.   5. nice and tasty.   6. short and fat

7. young and happy   8. tired and dirty   9. wet and windy

10. rich and famous   11. nice and sunny   12. hot and angry

Chapter Two

Word Groups

1. **Learn words in groups.**

   There are thousands of words in English. Try to learn words in groups. For example:

   > words for clothes
   > words for jobs
   > words for hobbies

2. **Make word groups in your vocabulary notebook.**

   In this chapter you must start to put words into groups. If you want, you can write the translation beside each word in the group.

2.1 Word groups – 1

furniture, family, colours, music

One way to build your vocabulary is to think of a topic and make a list of the words you know about that topic. When you find new words, you can add them to one of your lists.

In this exercise you will see words for four different topics. Put the words into four lists. Write the topic at the top of each list:

armchair	concert	opera singer	stool
bed	cousin	parents	table
brother-in-law	drums	play a tune	uncle
black	grandson.	pop song	violin
blue	green	red	white
chair	nephew.	sofa	yellow

1. *furniture*	2. *family*	3. *colours*	4. *music*
armchair	*brother-in-law*	*black*	*concert*
chair	grand son.	blue	pop song
bed	nephew	green	play a tune
sofa	prenents	red	opera singer
table	uncle	violin	nephew
		white	drums
		yellow	cousin
			concert

Can you think of any more words to add to the lists?

2.2 Word groups – 2

sport, drinks, clothes, weather

Put these words into four lists. Write the topic at the top of each list.

baseball team	heavy rain	pair of socks	sunny
bottle of wine	lemonade	pair of trousers	sunshine
blouse	long skirt	play volleyball	tennis court
cup of coffee	temperature	referee	warm coat
football stadium	mineral water	shower	win the match
glass of milk	orange juice	smart suit	windy

1. sport	2. drinks	3. clothes	4. weather
baseball team	bottle of wine	blouse	heavy rain
tennis court	cup of coffee	long skirt	sunshine
win the match	glass of milk		temperature
football stadium	mineral water	smart suit	heavy rain
play volleyball	orange juice	warm coat	sunny
pair of socks	lemonade		windy
pair of trousers	win the m...		
referee			
shower			

Can you think of any more words to add to the lists?

2.3 Days, months, seasons

Put these words into the lists in the correct order.

afternoon February May October Thursday
April Friday minute Saturday Tuesday
August hour Monday second Wednesday
autumn January month September week
day July morning spring winter
December June night summer year
evening March November Sunday

DAYS

1. *Monday*
2. Tuesday
3. wedneesday
4. Thursday
5. friday
6. saturday
7. sunday

MONTHS

1. *January*
2. february
3. march
4. April
5. may
6. June
7. July
8. August
9. september
10. October
11. November
12. December

SEASONS

1. *spring*
2. winter
3. autumn
4. summer

TIME

1. *second*
2. minute
3. hour
4. day
5. week
6. month
7. year

PARTS OF A DAY

1. *morning*
2. afternoon
3. evening
4. night

Notice that the days and months begin with CAPITAL LETTERS.

2.4 Men and women

When we use nouns to talk about men and women we usually use the same word, for example:

      doctor   cousin   student

Sometimes we have two different words, for example:

        son   daughter

Make three lists with these nouns:

husband	detective	princess	dancer	king
uncle	lawyer	receptionist	widow	girlfriend
wife	granddaughter	niece	reporter	artist
teacher	aunt	boyfriend	pilot	engineer
violinist	prince	manager	grandfather	grandson
grandmother	nephew	tourist	queen	mechanic

MEN	WOMEN	BOTH
uncle	*aunt*	*pilot*
husband	wife	teacher
granddaughter	grandmother	violinist
king	girlfriend	detective
grandson	widow	lawyer
queen	princess	tourist
boyfriend		manager
manager		artist
tourist		engineer
grandson		mechanic
		pilot
		reporter
		niece
		detective
		nephew

Can you add some more words for men and women to the lists?

2.5 School

Put these words in the correct lists. Can you think of any more words to add to the lists?

desk   good/bad at   mathematics   ruler   secondary school
dictionary headmistress   physics   take   schoolteacher
geography   lunch break   primary school   student   translate

SUBJECTS YOU LEARN	THINGS YOU USE
mathematics *secondary school* *schoolteacher* *geography* *physics*	*ruler* *dictionary* *desk*

PLACES WHERE YOU LEARN	PEOPLE
Primary school *secondary school* *school teacher* *head mistress*	

VERBS	OTHER USEFUL WORDS AND PHRASES
. . . . an exam . . . . into English	

Chapter Three

Topics

1. **Become a word collector!**

   Some people collect stamps. They put them in their stamp album.
   Why not become a **word** collector?

2. **When you collect words, decide where to put them.**

   This chapter will help you collect words in different topic areas, for example, holidays, numbers, jobs.

3. **Make word trees.**

   Look at page 26. This is a very useful way to organise words so that you can remember them. On this page all the words are connected - like all the branches of a tree.

4. **Use pictures.**

   Look at page 28. Some dictionaries have pictures to help you. Cut out pictures you like and put them in your vocabulary notebook, then write the words on the pictures.

3.1 Numbers

Exercise 1

Write the number in front of each word. Choose from these numbers:

0	1.5	2½	11	12	14	17	18	19	21	32	43	54
65	76	87	98	100	212	1,000	3,679	1,300,010				

1. ....19.... nineteen
2. ....18.... eighteen
3. ....87.... eighty-seven
4. ....11.... eleven
5. ....54.... fifty-four
6. ....43.... forty-three
7. ....14.... fourteen
8. ....100.... a (one) hundred
9. ....12.... a dozen
10. ....98.... ninety-eight

11. ....1·5.... one point five
12. ....17.... seventeen
13. ....76.... seventy-six
14. ....65.... sixty-five
15. ....32.... thirty-two
16. ....1,000.... a thousand
17. ....21.... twenty-one
18. ....2½.... two and a half
19. ....212.... two hundred and twelve
20. ....0.... zero

21. ..3,679.. three thousand, six hundred and seventy-nine
22. 1,300,010. one million, three hundred thousand and ten

Now cover the words and say the numbers.

Exercise 2

Write the correct word next to each number. Choose from these words:

eighth   first   second   thirty-first   twenty-seventh   fifteenth   fourth
third   twelfth   twenty-third   fifth   ninth   thirtieth   twentieth

1. 1st .first.......
2. 2nd .second......
3. 3rd ..third......
4. 4th ..fourth......
5. 5th ..fifth......
6. 8th ...eighth......
7. 9th ..ninth....

8. 12th ..twelfth.....
9. 15th fifteenth....
10. 20th twentieth
11. 23rd twenty-third
12. 27th twenty-seventh
13. 30th thirtieth....
14. 31st thirty-first

3.2 Dates

Exercise 1

Notice how we say dates in English:

1601	1999	2,000
sixteen oh one	nineteen ninety nine	the year two thousand

First match up the following. Then write the dates in words:

a. 1789   b. 1989   c. 1945   d. 1969

1. The first man on the moon _1989_ nineteen eighty nine
2. The start of the French Revolution _1789_ seventeen eighty nine
3. The end of the 2nd World War _1945_ nineteen forty five
4. The end of the Berlin Wall _1989_ nineteen eighty nine
5. The next Olympic Games _1969_ nineteen sixty nine

Exercise 2

Notice how we say dates:

13th Nov = the thirteenth of November

May 17th = May the seventeenth

How do you say these dates?

1. 1st Jan. (New Year's Day) . . . .
2. Feb. 29th (Every 4 years!) . . . .
3. 4th July (US Independence Day) . . . .
4. Dec. 24th (Christmas Eve) . . . .
5. Your birthday . . . .
6. A national holiday in your country . . . .
7. A special date for you . . . .

For May 17th Americans may also say: May seventeenth.

3.3 Time

You can say: three fifty   OR   ten to four

Write the times under each clock or watch:

1. . . . .

2. . . . .

3. . . . .

4. . . . .

5. . . . .

6. . . . .

7. . . . .

8. . . . .

9. . . . .

10. nearly . . . .

11. just after . . . . . .

12. almost . . . .

Notice that for train and aeroplane times you often say:

| 13.50 | thirteen fifty | 16.30 | sixteen thirty |
| 12.00 | twelve noon | 19.00 | nineteen hundred hours |

3.4 Places and prepositions

Exercise 1
Match the first half of the sentence on the left with the second half on the right. Use each half once only. Write your answers in the boxes.

1. You can park your car
2. You can study engineering
3. You can catch the fast train
4. You can have a room
5. You can get to work
6. You can have breakfast
7. You can send a fax
8. You can listen to the news

a. at university.
b. from this office.
c. on the radio.
d. in the first floor restaurant.
f. in the space next to mine.
g. on the fourth floor.
h. from the central station.
i. on the bus.

1	a	2	b	3	C	4	d	5	g	6	d	7	l	8	C

Exercise 2
Now do the same with these sentences.

1. You can improve your vocabulary
2. You can visit my aunt
3. You can live more cheaply
4. You can play basketball
5. You can drive to work
6. You can get new lenses
7. You can cross
8. You can't wear that dress

a. out in the country.
b. in the gym if you book it.
c. at her flat in Washington.
d. at the optician's in an hour.
f. at the traffic lights.
g. in my car if you want.
h. at the party!
i. on your own or in class.

1	i	2	C	3		4		5		6		7	f	8	h

3.5 People

Choose the best word to complete each sentence:

1. Margaret is my best .....*friend*..... I tell her everything.
   a. woman b. friend c. pet d. enemy

2. Excuse me. Can you tell me the way to the town hall?
   > I'm afraid not. I'm a .*tourist*. around here.
   a. conductor b. foreigner c. tourist d. stranger

3. They invited over 50 .*guests*.. to their daughter's wedding.
   a. guests b. hosts c. nieces d. priests

4. Excuse me, sir. Are you the .*owner*.. of this car?
   a. stranger b. owner c. pilot d. rider

5. Louise is a .*piano*... in our National Orchestra.
   a. piano b. florist c. violin d. violinist

6. The *mechanic*. at the garage said my car needed a new engine.
   a. athlete b. mechanic c. officer d. engineer

7. Good morning, ..*sir*...... I'm the manager. How can I help you?
   a. boy b. man c. mister d. sir

8. Michelle is a *customer*. so it's difficult for her to understand
   what people say if they speak very fast.
   a. beginner b. customer c. starter d. winner

9. Trevor works as a shop *assistant*. in a big store.
   a. assistant b. attendant c. brother d. instructor

10. My *mother-in-law* .... was never happy about me marrying her daughter.
    a. mother-in-law b. uncle c. nephew d. stepfather

11. Joe's doctor wasn't sure what was wrong with him so she sent him
    to a *specialist* at the hospital.
    a. principal b. specialist c. manager d. writer

12. The steward served coffee to the first-class *passengers* .
    a. assistants b. attendants c. passengers d. pilots

13. That *journalist* wants to write about you in his newspaper.
    a. coach b. cook c. journalist d. professor

14. A *babysitter* looks after our children when we go out for the evening.
    a. babysitter b. butcher c. cleaner d. disc jockey

24

3.6 Hobbies

One way to group your vocabulary when you think of a subject is to draw a diagram like the one on this page. As you will see, it shows only some of the possible words. Can you think of some more?

Put these words into the diagram:

| camera | horror | referee | take | cowboy | lose |
| shorts | video | guitar | penalty | stadium | violin |

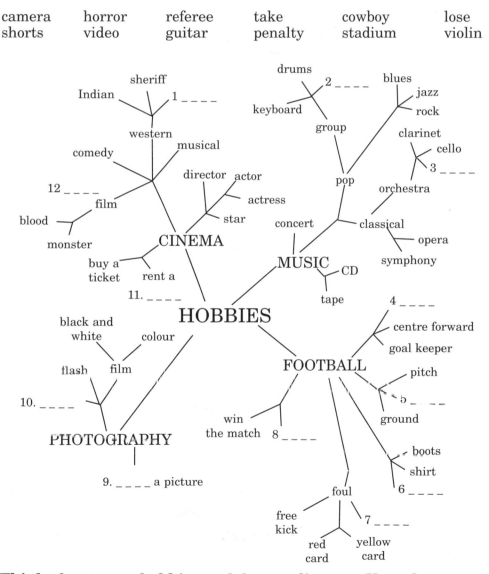

Think about your hobbies and draw a diagram. Use a large piece of paper!

3.7 Holidays

Put these words into the diagram:

airport   caravan   guide book   restaurant   swimming
aspirin   credit card   pool   single room   train
bike   disco   receptionist   suitcase   yacht

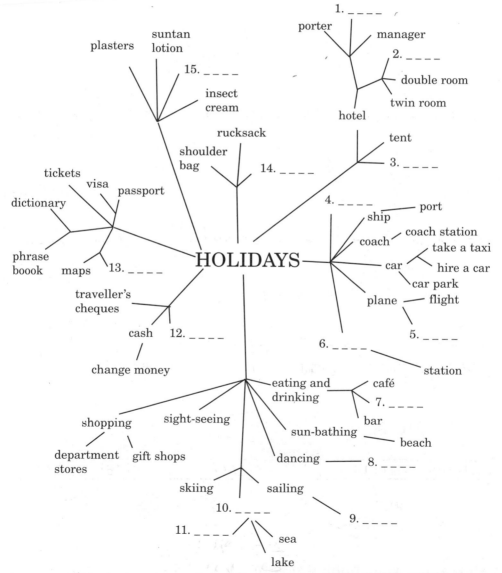

Can you think of any more words that could go in the diagram?

3.8 Jobs

Put each word under the correct picture.

car mechanic *13*   footballer *9*   nurse *2*   priest *11*   teacher *5*
tourist guide *6*   hairdresser *14*   office worker *15*   sailor *7*   cook *4*
shop assistant *10*   librarian *18*   pilot *3*   doctor *1*   waiter *20*
factory worker *8*   lorry driver *16*   plumber   taxi driver *12*   vet *19*

1. doctor worker
2. nurse
3. pilot
4. cook
5. teacher
6. tourist guide
7. sailor
8. factory worker
9. footballer
10. shop assistant
11. priest
12. taxi driver
13. car mechanic
14. hairdresser
15. office worker
16. lorry driver
17. plumber guide
18. librarian
19. vet
20. waiter

3.9 Transport

Put the correct sentence under each picture.

We hired a car.   We came on our bikes. 8   We came on foot. 6
4 We came by train.   We got the car ferry. 5   We took the underground. 9
We flew.   We took a taxi. 3   We went by bus. 2

1. we flew
2. we went by bus
3. we took a taxi
4. we come by tein
5. we got the car freey
6. we come on frot
7. we hired a car
8. we come on our bikes
9. we took the underground

Now fill in the following words:

coaches   walk   cycle   by boat   by plane

1. If you fly, you go . . . by plane . . . .
2. Buses for long journeys are usually called . . . by boat . . . . .
3. If you go on a ferry, you can also say . . . by plane . . . .
4. If you go on foot, you. . . . . cycle . . .
5. If you go by bike, you . . . coaches . . . . .

28

3.10 My day

Write the correct sentence under each picture.

We kissed goodnight.   I was busy all afternoon.   I went to the dentist. 9
I got up at 7.30. 1   I had a meeting at 9. 4   I met Mark for lunch. 6
I had a shower. 2   We had dinner. 8   I waited for the bus. 3

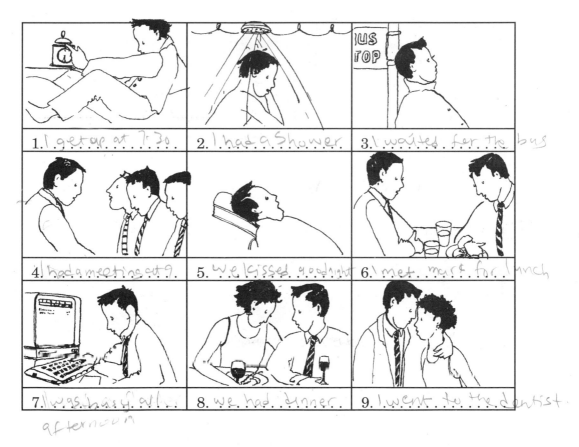

1. I get up at 7.30.   2. I had a Shower.   3. I waited for the bus

4. I had a meeting at 9.   5. We kissed goodnight   6. I met mark for lunch

7. I was busy all   8. we had dinner.   9. I went to the dentist.
afternoon

In the pictures what words come after 'have'?

have a s _ _ _ _ _   have a _ _ _ _ _ _ g   have _ _ _ _ e _

Which 8 of these can follow HAVE?

a sandwich   a headache   cold   a good time   a coffee

a problem   hunger   an idea   a bad throat   a beer

3.11 In the street

Put the correct word under each picture.

road sign   lamp post   motorbike   pram   phone box
bus stop   litter bin   pavement   bike   traffic lights
crossing   lorry   policeman   van   public toilet (loo)

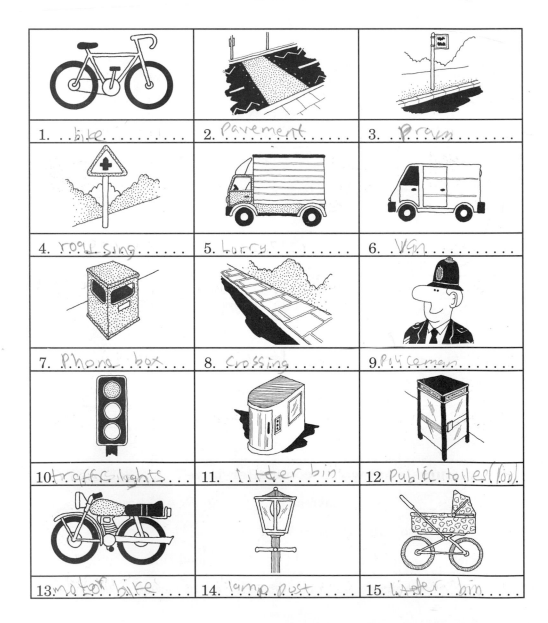

1. ...bike.........
2. Pavement......
3. ...Pram.......
4. road sing......
5. Lorry.........
6. ..Van.........
7. Phone box...
8. Crossing.......
9. Policeman......
10. traffic lights...
11. ..Litter bin..
12. Public toiles(loo).
13. motor bike...
14. lamp post....
15. Litter bin....

3.12 Common things – 1

Write the correct word under each picture.

comb	pencil	credit card	wallet	envelope
key	glasses	calculator	coins	scissors
pen	stamp	magazine	notes	file
watch	clock	toothbrush	cheque	contact lenses

1. clock
2. Pen
3. Key
4. notes
5. files
6. Calculator
7. toothbrush
8. glasses
9. Pencil
10. watch
11. Comb
12. credit card
13. Cheque
14. wallet
15. Contact lenses
16. Coinsie
17. Magazine
18. scissors
19. envelope
20. stamp

3.13 Common things – 2

Write the names of these things under the correct picture.

camera   personal CD   radio/cassette recorder
camcorder   stereo system   personal stereo
car stereo   headphones   mobile phone

1. moble phone

2. head phones

3. radio cassette recorder

4. car stereo

5. Stereon system

6. Camera

7. Personal CD

8. Personal stereo

9. Camera

3.14 Fruit and vegetables

Write each of the following words under the correct picture.

apple   beans   banana   lettuce   cucumber   onions
peas   peach   cabbage   orange   potatoes   lemon
pear   grapes   carrot   cherries   tomatoes   pineapple

FRUIT

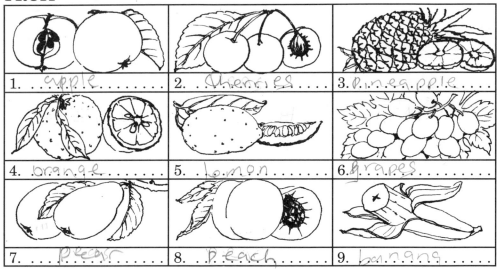

1. apple
2. cherries
3. pineapple
4. orange
5. lemon
6. grapes
7. pear
8. peach
9. banana

VEGETABLES

10. peas
11. lettuce
12. potatoes
13. carrot
14. beans
15. onions

SALAD

16. cabbage
17. cucumber
18. tomatoes

3.15 Sports

Write each of the following sports under the correct picture:

cycling	golf	sailing	basketball	American football
fishing	skiing	skating	swimming	riding
football	tennis	surfing	windsurfing	table tennis

1. football
2. tennis
3. golf
4. skating
5. skiing
6. Cycling
7. Fishing
8. sailing
9. windsurfing
10. swimming
11. Table tennis
12. Surfing
13. riding
14. basketball
15. American football

3.16 Clothes

Write each of the following words under the correct picture.

anorak	coat	jacket	skirt	T-shirt	jumper/sweater/pullover
boots	dress	scarf	trainers	tights	knickers/pants
bra	shirt	shoe	socks	trousers	track-suit
cap	hat	shorts	suit	underpants	jeans

1. T.shirt
2. shoe
3. shorts
4. trainers
5. dress
6. skirt
7. bra
8. tights
9. anorak
10. coas
11. Jacket
12. track-suit
13. Jeans
14. Scarf
15. Suit
16. trousers
17. Cap
18. T-shirt
19. boots
20. Shorts
21. Jumper/ sweater/Pullover
22. hat
23. Underpants
24. knickers/pants

3.17 Restaurant food

**Here is a list of food you could find on a menu in a restaurant.
Put the words in the correct place on the menu.**

ice cream	vegetable soup	roast pork	peas
lobster	apple pie	sole	yoghurt
chocolate mousse	rump steak	fruit juice	beans
roast potatoes	cauliflower	baked potato	carrots
lamb cutlets	Scottish salmon	mashed potato	fruit salad
grilled trout	roast chicken	French fries	

STARTERS

. . . .

MAIN COURSES

FISH/SHELLFISH	MEAT	VEGETABLES	POTATOES
. . . .	*roast chicken*	*beans*	*baked potato*
. . . .	*French fries*	*vegetable soup*	*roast potatos*
. . . .	. . . .	*carrots*	*mashed potato*
. . . .	. . . .	*fruit salad*	*roast potatoes*
	beautiful		

DESSERTS

. . . .

. . . .

**When you have finished this, there should be one space left for
a dessert. What is your favourite dessert? Find out what it is in
English and write it in the last space.**

Chapter Four

Word Formation

1. **You can make words from words.**

   Many words belong to families which are related, for example:

You study	>	science
The person	>	a scientist
The adjective	>	scientific

2. **Try to build words.**

   When you learn a new word, look in your dictionary and find its relations! Write them in your vocabulary notebook.

3. **Make word families.**

   You will learn a lot of new words and you will learn how to make new words by studying words in their families.

4.1 Making adjectives

Complete each sentence with a form of the word in brackets, for example:

It's too . *windy* . . . to wear a hat today.   (WIND)

The new word will end in *-ed*, *-ful*, *-ing* or *-y*.

1. Be _careful_ . ! You might break something!   (CARE)

2. If it's _sunny_ . . tomorrow, let's go to the beach.   (SUN)

3. Lenny looked very _surprising_ when he saw us.   (SURPRISE)

4. We've got some very _surprising_ news for you.   (SURPRISE)

5. We watched a very _funny_ . . show on television
    last night.   (FUN)

6. Mum gets _worried_ when Jill is so late.   (WORRY)

7. In _stormy_ . weather like this the yachts
    usually stay in the harbour.   (STORM)

8. In my country most _married_ . men don't wear
    a ring.   (MARRY)

9. I went to an _interesting_ talk about finding a job.   (INTEREST)

10. Bye! Have a _wonderful_ holiday!   (WONDER)

11. Sheila lives in a very _beautiful_ . part of
    the country.   (BEAUTY)

12. John usually feels _sleepy_ . after a big meal.   (SLEEP)

13. A calculator can be very _useful_ . if you work
    in a shop.   (USE)

14. Gina was very _embarrassed_ when people stared   (EMBARRASS)
    at her new hairdo.

15. It's really _tiring_ . sitting at a computer all day.   (TIRE)

16. As the plane came nearer the airport, we all   (EXCITE)
    got very _excited_ .

4.2 Making nouns

Change each word in brackets to complete the sentence, for example:

I've got an *invitation* to a party tonight.   (INVITE)

The words end in *-er, -ing* or *-tion*.

1. We have an electric *cooker* in our kitchen but my mother has gas.   (COOK)

2. My office is in a big *building* near the bus station.   (BUILD)

3. Have you got any *information* about flights to Los Angeles?   (INFORM)

4. What's the *meaning* of the word "exhausted" ?   (MEAN)

5. Can you help me? I don't understand how this video *recorder* works.   (RECORD)

6. The *beginning* of the book is good but it gets boring.   (BEGIN)

7. I'm going to town to do some *shopping*. Do you want to come with me?   (SHOP)

8. We went to an interesting *exhibition* of old cars at a large house in the country.   (EXHIBIT)

9. Have you got a *hanger* I can put my jacket on?   (HANG)

10. I'm afraid *smoking* is not permitted in this room.   (SMOKE)

11. We made this ice-cream with our own ice-cream *maker*.   (MAKE)

12. Stop! Come back! You're going in the wrong *direction*!   (DIRECT)

13. What time does the *meeting* start this evening?   (MEET)

14. Juan bought a Spanish *translation* of Animal Farm.   (TRANSLATE)

15. Is there any ice cream in the *freezer*?   (FREEZE)

16. Now we have central *heating*, the house is much warmer.   (HEAT)

17. Sarah has over ten thousand stamps in her *collection*.   (COLLECT)

18. There's a *painting* of a horse on the wall by Mary's bed.   (PAINT)

4.3 Nouns for people

When you look at a word in a dictionary, see if you can make other words from it, for example:

farm > farmer   visit > visitor

Write the word for the person after the words below. Each new word ends with *-er* or *-or*.

1. act   _actor_
2. bake   _baker_
3. collect   _collector_
4. direct   _director_
5. drive   _driver_
6. farm   _farmer_
7. garden   _gardener_
8. inspect   _inspector_
9. instruct   _instrcctor_
10. manage   _manager_

11. operate   _operator_
12. play   _player_
13. report   _reporter_
14. ride   _rider_
15. run   _runner_
16. sail   _sailor_
17. teach   _teacher_
18. translate   _Translator_
19. visit   _visitor_
20. work   _worker_

Now use some of the nouns to complete these sentences:

1. Are you sure this taxi _driver_ knows where he's going?

2. My bank _Manager_ doesn't want to lend me any more money.

3. I'm a stamp _collector_ in my spare time.

4. A newspaper _reporter_ wants to ask you about your accident.

5. A good football _player_ can make a lot of money.

6. I think my driving _Instructor_ was surprised when I passed my test.

40

4.4 Countries - nationalities

In this exercise you will see a list of countries and nationalities.
Put in the missing words. Choose from these words:

Brazilian	Canada	Chinese	Finnish	French	German
Greece	Hungary	Ireland	Japan	Lebanese	Mexican
Omani	Polish	Portugal	Russia	Scotland	Spanish
Switzerland	Taiwanese	Thai	Turkey	Vietnam	Wales

-an		-ish	
Brazil	*Brazilian*	Finland	*Finnish*
Canada	Canadian	*Ireland*	Irish
Germany	*German*	Poland	*Polish*
Hungary	Hungarian	*Scotland*	Scottish
Mexico	*Mexican*	Spain	*Spanish*
Russia	Russian	*Turkey*	Turkish
. . . . .	. . . . .	. . . . .	. . . . .
. . . . .	. . . . .	. . . . .	. . . . .
. . . . .	. . . . .	. . . . .	. . . . .
. . . . .	. . . . .	. . . . .	. . . . .

-ese		others	
China	*CHINESE*	France	*French*
Japan	Japanese	*Greece*	Greek
Lebanon	*Lebanese*	Oman	*Omani*
Portugal	Portuguese	*Switzerland*	Swiss
Taiwan	*Taiwanese*	Thailand	*Thai*
Vietnam	Vietnamese	*Wales*	Welsh
. . . . .	. . . . .	. . . . .	. . . . .
. . . . .	. . . . .	. . . . .	. . . . .
. . . . .	. . . . .	. . . . .	. . . . .
. . . . .	. . . . .	. . . . .	. . . . .

**Is your country in one of the lists? If not, put it in the right list.
Can you think of any more countries to add to the lists?**

4.5 Word families

You will need a dictionary to help you with this exercise. Look up the word in CAPITALS in your dictionary and near it you should find a word from the same family to complete the sentence.

1. FLY
I want to be a pilot. I'm having . . . . lessons.   **adjective**

2. DAY
Is the Times the best . . . . newspaper?   **adjective**

3. ILL
Sam's got a very serious . . . .   **noun**

4. ANGRY
Pat's . . . . didn't go away. It got worse!   **noun**

5. COMPOSE
Some people think Mozart was the greatest . . . .   **noun**

6. FAULT
My new radio is . . . .   **adjective**

7. POLITICS
Greg's a left-wing . . . .   **noun**

8. STORM
It was very . . . . last night.   **adjective**

9. POSSIBLE
There are lots of . . . .   **noun**

10. SHORT
They want to . . . . our lunch break!   **verb**

11. HEALTH
A . . . . mind in a . . . . body.   **adjective**

12. HEAR
Sue's . . . . was damaged when the bomb went off.   **noun**

Chapter Five

Spelling and Pronunciation

1. A word is more than its meaning.

When you learn a new word, you learn its meaning and perhaps you also translate it into your own language. At the same time, try to learn its pronunciation and its spelling.

2. Phonetic symbols.

In all good dictionaries every word is given in phonetics / fənetɪks/.
If you learn these symbols, it will make it easier to learn the pronunciation of words.

5.1 Vowel sounds

It is sometimes difficult to know how to spell a new English word you hear or to know how to pronounce a word you see. It is important to learn the phonetic symbols you find in your dictionary so that when you meet a new word you know how to say it. This exercise will help you practise some of the phonetic symbols and show you different ways of spelling them.

Put the words into the correct list for their vowel sound:

boot	here	new	steak	toe	wear
chair	know	phone	their	top	what
cheer	make	rain	they	two	where
dear	near	shop	toast	want	you

1. /ɒ/
(lot)

. . . .

. . . .

. . . .

. . . .

2. /uː/
(too)

. . . .

. . . .

. . . .

. . . .

3. /eə/
(there)

. . . .

. . . .

. . . .

. . . .

4. /eɪ/
(say)

. . . .

. . . .

. . . .

. . . .

5. /ɪə/
(ear)

. . . .

. . . .

. . . .

. . . .

6. /əʊ/
(go)

. . . .

. . . .

. . . .

. . . .

5.2 Same sound – 1

There are some words in English which we pronounce in the same way but which have a different spelling and a different meaning, for example:

    it's   its   there   they're   their

It is a good idea to make a list of any words like this and to check that you have the correct spelling each time you use one of them.

Use these words to complete the pairs of sentences. Use each pair once only.

buy/by	it's/its	sea/see	too/two
hear/here	right/write	son/sun	who's/whose

1. a. I like swimming and my friend does, ...

   b. Anne has . . . . children, a girl and a boy.

2. a. My . . . . , Bob, works in a car factory.

   b. When the . . . . shines, everyone feels much better.

3. a. They live by the . . . . and often go sailing.

   b. It's too dark in here! I can't . . . . anything!

4. a. Oh dear! I think . . . . raining!

   b. The plant I bought lost all . . . . leaves.

5. a. I'm going to the shops to . . . . a birthday card.

   b. Could you sit over there, ... the window?

6. a. Don't speak so softly. I can't . . . . you.

   b. Henry, come . . . . a moment, please.

7. a. My house is the third one on the . . . .

   b. If you want to come, please . . . . your name on the list.

8. a. I have a friend . . . . studying at university.

   b. I have a friend . . . . father is a journalist.

5.3 Same sound – 2

Use each pair of words once only to complete the pairs of sentences:

fair/fare	meat/meet	some/sum	wait/weight
hour/our	pair/pear	their/there	weak/week
knew/new	passed/past	there/they're	wood/would

1. a. We . . . . the sports club on our way home.

   b. We went . . . . the sports club on our way home.

2. a. I thought I . . . . the answer but I was wrong.

   b. What do you think of Neil's . . . . motorbike?

3. a. The students are worried about . . . . exams.

   b. Why aren't . . . . more plays on television?

4. a. You should work for an . . . . and then take a break.

   b. We're very pleased with . . . . new video.

5. a. This chair is made of . . . ., not plastic.

   b. Milly . . . . really like to go out with Paul.

6. a. She's a vegetarian. She doesn't eat . . . .

   b. Shall we . . . . outside the cinema at half past?

7. a. I have a terrible headache and feel very . . . .

   b. Only one more . . . . and then it's my holiday!

8. a. We need . . . . more butter.

   b. Can you do this . . . . ? I'm hopeless at maths!

9. a. Could you put the bags over . . . . in the corner?

   b. Who are those people? - I think . . . . tourists.

10. a. He's quite tall and has . . . . hair.

    b. How much is the cheapest . . . . to New York?

11. a. I'd like to buy a . . . . of trousers.

    b. Which would you prefer - a . . . . or a banana?

12. a. I usually . . . . for the bus near the town hall.

    b. What's the . . . . of your luggage? - 20 kilos.

5.4 Rhymes

In this exercise you will see lists of four words. One of the words does not rhyme with the others (does not sound the same). Draw a circle around the odd one out.

1. call	fall	(shall)	wall
2. clown	down	own	town
3. feel	meal	she'll	well
4. above	glove	love	move
5. cow	go	know	throw
6. gun	one	phone	sun
7. bought	caught	coat	sort
8. clear	dear	hear	pear
9. hair	here	there	wear
10. cost	most	post	roast
11. after	daughter	quarter	shorter
12. eat	great	hate	wait
13. boot	route	shoot	shout
14. my	pie	tea	tie
15. do	new	no	through
16. arm	calm	farm	warm
17. laid	paid	said	stayed
18. great	late	wait	white

5.5 Stress patterns

In this exercise put each word in the right list for its stress pattern. The sign ▼ shows the main stress, for example:

▼ ○
music

again
another
April
banana
begin
between

○ ▼
arrive

breakfast
certainly
December
difficult
easy
eleven

▼ ○ ○
photograph

enjoy
example
holiday
hospital
hotel
husband

○ ▼ ○
mechanic

Japan
manager
musician
sweater
telephone
traffic

1. ▼ ○

again
April
begin
enjoy
hotel
Japan

2. ○ ▼

eleven
banana

3. ▼ ○ ○

4. ○ ▼ ○

Chapter Six

Word Partnerships

1. **Words go together in special ways.**

   In English we normally say:
   > I made a mistake.

   We don't say:
   > I did a mistake.

   The normal verb we use with *mistake* is *make*.
   Make a mistake is a 'word partnership'.

2. **When you learn a word, learn the words that go with it.**

   This is important. Single words are not often used alone. Your English will improve if you start to learn more and more word partnerships.

6.1 Verb + noun

It is important when you learn vocabulary to see how words go together. It is better to learn verb and noun partnerships, for example, than to learn the noun on its own.

Exercise 1
Match a verb on the left with a noun on the right. Use each word once only. Write your answers in the boxes.

1. do		a the bell	1	d
2. listen to		b. a flat	2	f
3. post		c. hands	3	e
4. rent		d. your homework	4	b
5. ring		e. a letter	5	a
6. shake		f. the radio	6	c
7. tell		g. television	7	h
8. watch		h. the truth	8	g

Exercise 2
Now do the same with these words:

1. brush		a. a bus	1	e
2. catch		b. cards	2	a
3. change		c. the door	3	g
4. cross		d. your English	4	h
5. improve		e. your hair	5	d
6. lock		f. glasses	6	b
7. play		g. your mind	7	c
8. wear		h. the road	8	f

Now use some of the phrases to complete these sentences:

1. We usually *shake hands* when we meet people for the first time.
2. Jill has to *wear glasses* because she can't see very well.
3. Have you got a stamp? I want to *post a letter* to my parents.
4. Building your vocabulary is the best way to *improve your English*

6.2 Adjective + noun

Exercise 1

Match an adjective on the left with a noun on the right.
Be careful! Some adjectives can go with more than one noun but you must use each word once only. Write your answers in the boxes.

1.	comfortable		a.	chair
2.	dark		b.	disco
3.	empty		c.	game
4.	exciting		d.	glass
5.	heavy		e.	hair
6.	long		f.	man
7.	noisy		g.	suitcase
8.	single		h.	time

1	a
2	e
3	d
4	c
5	g
6	h
7	b
8	f

Exercise 2

Now do the same with these words:

1.	blonde		a.	day
2.	careful		b.	driver
3.	delicious		c.	hair
4.	interesting		d.	lesson
5.	loud		e.	meal
6.	married		f.	mistake
7.	silly		g.	noise
8.	sunny		h.	woman

1	c
2	b
3	e
4	d
5	g
6	h
7	f
8	a

Now use some of the phrases to complete these sentences:

1. On a sunny day like this I usually go for a swim in the sea.
2. That isn't a very comfortable chair! Why don't you sit here?
3. Sometimes you have to wait a long time before the bus comes.
4. I knew the answer, but I still made a silly mistake

51

6.3 Useful verbs – 1

Exercise 1
Put the correct verb under each picture. Choose from this list:

dance	miss	read	throw
drink	open	ride	walk
eat	paint	smile	write

1. read
2. eat
3. paint
4. ride
5. write
6. smile
7. dance
8. miss
9. drink
10. throw
11. open
12. walk

Exercise 2
Now put verbs from the list in front of these words:

1. open the door
2. Paint a picture
3. eat a pizza
4. read the paper
5. throw a ball
6. ride a bike
7. write/read a letter
8. miss the bus

52

6.4 Useful verbs – 2

Exercise 1
Put the correct verb under each picture. Choose from this list:

climb	cut	fall	run
close	draw	jump	sing
cry	drive	kick	wash

1. drive
2. sing
3. wash
4. cut
5. draw
6. fall
7. close
8. jump
9. kick
10. run
11. climb
12. cry

Exercise 2
Now put verbs from the list in front of these words:

1. wash your face
2. sing a song
3. drive a car
4. draw a picture
5. kick a football
6. climb a mountain
7. cut your nails
8. close the door

53

6.7 Two-word expressions

Sometimes in English you can put two words together to form a common expression, for example:

swimming pool   car park   orange juice

You should look for expressions like these and add them to your vocabulary lists.

Join one word from the left with one from the right to make a two-word partnership. Use each word once only. Write your answers in the boxes.

1. ice		a. book		1	d
2. driving		b. card		2	h
3. summer		c. centre		3	g
4. writing		d. cream		4	j
5. weather		e. floor		5	f
6. identity		f. forecast		6	b
7. football		g. holiday		7	i
8. diamond		h. licence		8	m
9. shop		i. match		9	o
10. soap		j. paper		10	k
11. shopping		k. powder		11	c
12. cheque		l. recorder		12	a
13. cassette		m. ring		13	l
14. ground		n. ticket		14	e
15. theatre		o. window		15	n

Now complete each sentence with one of the expressions:

1. Last July we went to Rome for our ....Summer holiday....
2. What would you like - the ...ice cream... or the fruit salad?
3. The ...weather forecast... is for rain and then snow in the evening.
4. We had a room on the ...ground floor... so we didn't have to use the lift.

56

Chapter Seven

Situations

1. **Fixed expressions are important in conversations.**

   Vocabulary is not just words. Fixed expressions can be very important - especially in conversations. Here are some examples:

   > How are you?
   > Nice to meet you.
   > Excuse me . . . . . .

2. **Try to speak friendly English.**

   Conversational expressions are very important to show other people that you are friendly and polite. You can seem rude if you do not know the correct phrase in a particular situation, so fixed expressions are very important.

7.1 Everyday situations

Match each of these answers with the sentences in the pictures:

She doesn't feel very well.
Certainly. Here you are.
Oh no! What shall we do?
Nothing special. Why?

Yes, I am. Can I help you?
Thank you. It's nice to be here.
Thank you. The same to you.
That's all right. It doesn't matter.

Excuse me, Are you the manager?

1. Yes, I am. Can I help

What are you doing this evening?

2. Nothing special. why

Have a nice weekend.

3. Thankyuo. The same for. you

Could you pass me the salt, please.

4. Certaly. Here yuo are

I'm sorry I'm late.

It doesn't matter
5. That his all right....

Welcome to Sydney.

6. Thankyuo. it is nice to be here

The door is locked!

7. Certoly. Here yuo are

What's the matter with Ann?

8. She does sheel very well

7.2 Around town

Match the sentences on the left with the places on the right:

1. Three stamps for Russia, please.
2. A table for two, please.
3. I'd like my eyes tested, please.
4. A day return to Oxford, please.
5. Six oranges, please.
6. A bottle of aspirin, please.
7. A small brown loaf, please.
8. Not too short at the back, please.
9. A single room with bath, please.
10. The Sunday Times, please.

a. in a hotel
b. in the newsagent's
c. at the hairdresser's
d. in the baker's
e. in a restaurant
f. at the station
g. in the post office
h. in the optician's
i. in the chemist's
j. in the greengrocer's

Write your answers here:

| 1 | g | 2 | e | 3 | h | 4 | f | 5 | j | 6 | i | 7 | d | 8 | c | 9 | a | 10 | b |

Can you think of any more things people say in these places?

A single to Gatwick, please.

. . . .

. . . .

. . . .

. . . .

7.3 At a restaurant

Conversation 1

Use these phrases to complete the first part of the conversation:

for me, too	I'd like	soup of the day
What would you like	Are you ready	

Waiter	(1) . . . . to order now?
Andy	Yes, I think so. (2) . . . . to start with, Helen?
Helen	What's the (3) . . . . ?
Waiter	Vegetable, madam.
Helen	O.K. Vegetable soup for me, please.
Andy	And (4) . . . ., please.
Waiter	And for the main course, Madam?
Helen	(5) . . . . roast chicken with mashed potato and peas, please.
Andy	And I'll have spaghetti bolognese.

Conversation 2

Now do the same with the second part of the conversation.

What a pity	Thank you very much	I'm very sorry
something to drink	How would you like it	

Waiter	(1) . . . . but I'm afraid we haven't got any left, sir.
Andy	Oh dear! (2) . . . . ! Then I'll have the rump steak.
Waiter	(3) . . . ., sir?
Andy	Medium, please.
Waiter	And which vegetables would you like with that, sir?
Andy	French fries and peas, please.
Waiter	Would you like (4) . . . . ?
Helen	A glass of red wine, please.
Andy	And a bottle of mineral water for me, please.
Waiter	(5) . . . .

60

7.4 Asking the way

Conversation 1
Complete the conversation by using these words:

I'm afraid not	Pardon	Could you tell me the way
Good idea	Excuse me	Why don't you ask

Mike   (1) . . . .

Silvia   Yes?

Mike   (2) . . . . to the nearest post office, please?

Silvia   (3) . . . . ?

Mike   Do you know where the nearest post office is?

Silvia   No, (4). I'm a stranger around here.

           (5) . . . . that policeman over there?

Mike   Oh yes. (6) . . . . Thanks.

Conversation 2
Now do the same with this conversation.

the second on the right	how to get to	You're welcome
just after a supermarket	turn left	of course

Mike   Excuse me. Could you tell me (1) . . . . the nearest post office, please?

PC Stone   Yes, (2) . . . . Go down this street and

             (3) . . . . , at the traffic lights. Take

             (4) . . . . That's the road with a cinema on

             the corner. The post office is about a hundred metres along

             the road on the right, (5) . . . .

Mike   So that's left at the traffic lights, then second right. Thanks very much.

PC Stone   (6) . . . .

7.5 At a party

Exercise 1

Here are some conversations at a party. Match the parts on the left with the parts on the right. Use each part of the conversation once only.
Write your answers in the boxes.

1. What do you do?
2. How far is that from here?
3. What nationality are you?
4. Hello! My name's Mike Smith.
5. What do you do in your spare time?
6. Where do you come from?
7. Where do you live?
8. How do you spell that?

a. In a flat in Baker Street.
b. I like taking photos.
c. Mexico.
d. T-H-O-M-S-O-N.
e. Pleased to meet you.
f. Austrian.
g. About 6 kilometres.
h. I'm a journalist.

1		2		3		4		5		6		7		8	

Exercise 2

Now do the same for this exercise:

1. What star sign are you?
2. How are you?
3. I'll have to go in a minute.
4. What's the time?
5. Have you got a light?
6. Hello, Sarah.
7. Thanks for inviting me.
8. What would you like to drink?

a. What? So soon?
b. About half past eleven.
c. Thanks for coming.
d. Just an orange juice, please.
e. Hi, Andy.
f. Fine thanks. And you?
g. Leo. What's yours?
h. No, I'm afraid not. I don't smoke.

1		2		3		4		5		6		7		8	

Chapter Eight

Word Grammar

1. **Grammar is words as well as rules.**

    When you think of grammar, you think of tenses and rules. But grammar is also about words - plurals, prepositions, nouns, adjectives, and the way these words go together. If you study the grammar of words, it will help your English.

2. **Put similar things together.**
    In your vocabulary notebook put things together in patterns, for example:

    > adjective + preposition
    > verb + at
    > verb + to

    This is another useful way of looking at grammar.

8.1 Plurals

Most nouns form their plural by adding 's', for example:
    book   books   shoe   shoes
With some nouns it is not so easy, for example:
    dress   dresses   family   families
It is a good idea to check the plural of every new noun you meet.

Exercise 1
Form the plural of these nouns:

1. baby . . . .
2. box . . . .
3. boy . . . .
4. child . . . .
5. class . . . .
6. day . . . .
7. factory . . . .

8. knife . . . .
9. leaf . . . .
10. lunch . . . .
11. man . . . .
12. tomato . . . .
13. tooth . . . .
14. woman . . . .

Exercise 2
Complete each of the sentences by using the plural form of the noun in brackets at the end:

1. More . . . . ? - No thanks. I really couldn't.   (STRAWBERRY)

2. Big . . . . make too much noise.   (LORRY)

3. All the . . . . except the 6B go to the town centre.   (BUS)

4. Let's take our . . . . to the park.   (SANDWICH)

5. Good evening, ... and . . . .   (LADY, GENTLEMAN)

6. My . . . . are really sore after all that walking.   (FOOT)

Can you think of any more plurals like those in the exercise?

8.2 Opposites – verbs

Match each verb with its opposite in the box.

1. agree	*disagree*	8. hate	. . . .	
2. ask	. . . .	9. land	. . . .	
3. borrow	. . . .	10. laugh	. . . .	
4. close	. . . .	11. leave	. . . .	
5. come down	. . . . . .	12. remember	. . . . . .	
6. find	. . . .	13. sell	. . . .	
7. finish	. . . .	14. take off	. . . .	

answer	lend
arrive	lose
buy	love
cry	open
disagree	put on
forget	start
go up	take off

Now complete each sentence with the pairs of words. Use each pair once only:

15. We expect the party to . . *finish/start* . . . . at about six.

16. Some shops . . . . at seven o'clock.

17. Why did you . . . . so much money?

18. I . . . . going to discos.

19. Where did you . . . . your watch? – In the restaurant.

20. The train should . . . . at five thirty.

21. Why can't you . . . . what she said?

22. How many postcards did you . . . . ?

23. James started to . . . . when he heard the news.

24. Does anybody else want to . . . . any questions?

25. I hope prices will . . . . soon.

26. Please . . . . that jacket. You look ridiculous.

27. What time does their plane . . . . ?

28. I . . . . with most of what Brian says.

8.3 Opposites – adjectives

Complete each sentence by using the opposite of the word in brackets. Choose from the words below. Use each word once.

bad	difficult	late	open
big	fast	left	tall
cold	first	long	young
expensive	high	new	wrong

1. Now this question is very . . . .   (EASY)

2. Be careful! The water is very . . . . !   (HOT)

3. I see you're wearing your . . . . jacket today. (OLD)

4. You're too . . . . to go to a disco.   (OLD)

5. Food is . . . . in this country.   (CHEAP)

6. I have some . . . . news for you.   (GOOD)

7. The . . . . thing I must do is phone my friend. (LAST)

8. It's a . . . . journey from here to the mountains. (SHORT)

9. Sandra's boyfriend is . . . . and has brown hair. (SHORT)

10. I usually travel on the . . . . train to the city. (SLOW)

11. All the windows upstairs are . . . .   (SHUT)

12. The bus is sometimes . . . . in the winter.   (EARLY)

13. How . . . . is Frank's car?   (SMALL)

14. Prices are often very . . . . in the summer.   (LOW)

15. Now lift your . . . . leg as high as possible.   (RIGHT)

16. How many questions did you get . . . . ?   (RIGHT)

Now find words in the exercise which could be opposite in meaning to:

17. dear   . . . .   21. hard   . . . .

18. correct   . . . .   22. quick   . . . .

19. freezing   . . . .   23. closed   . . . .

20. huge   . . . .   24. final   . . . .

8.4 Prepositions of place – 1

Put the following prepositions under the correct picture. Use each preposition once only.

outside	in	at	beside
through	under	over	down
behind	near	on	between

1. . . . . . . the moon

2. . . . . . . the top

3. . . . . . . the car

4. . . . . . . my back

5. . . . . . . the tent

6. . . . . . the keyhole

7. . . . . . . the hill

8. . . . . . . the hurdle

9. . . . . . . Parliament

10. . . . . . . the clock

11. . . . . . . the cars

12. . . . . . . Paris

8.5 Prepositions of place – 2

Choose the correct preposition:

1. Brian's staying with a friend . . . . number 6 London Road.
    a. at   b. on   c. up   d. through

2. Go . . . . that road and you'll see a No. 57 bus stop.
    a. between   b. at   c. across   d. around

3. Be careful! Don't fall . . . . the stairs. They're still wet.
    a. to   b. down   c. past   d. opposite

4. Graham sits . . . . Janet and Rita in music lessons.
    a. at   b. among   c. between   d. in

5. Turn left . . . . the traffic lights, then right.
    a. at   b. on   c. into   d. along

6. Walk . . . . the road as far as the park.
    a. at   b. along   c. through   d. around

7. We live . . . . Glasgow, not far from the city centre.
    a. at   b. among   c. in   d. on

8. You'll find the book . . . . the table, under the newspaper.
    a. at   b. in   c. on   d. back to

9. Malcolm lives in a large house . . . . Nelson Avenue.
    a. through   b. in   c. among   d. between

10. The office where I work is . . . . the town centre.
    a. on   b. near   c. along   d. across

11. Put your bag . . . . the chair. It'll be safe there.
    a. at   b. up   c. under   d. past

12. Our flat is . . . . the shop so we don't have far to go to work!
    a. on   b. above   c. back to   d. off

13. Take your feet . . . . the table! Who do you think you are?
    a. in front of   b. down   c. not far from   d. off

14. The station is . . . . the town centre so leave early!
    a. down   b. on   c. off   d. a long way from

15. Meet me . . . . the bus stop at a quarter to eight.
    a. over   b. at   c. across   d. through

8.6 Prepositions of time

at, in, on

Notice how we use the three prepositions:

AT	**a time** - at 6 o'clock
	a festival - at Christmas, Easter, Midsummer
	in the expressions - at night, at the moment, at the weekend
IN	**a month** - in October
	a year - in 1990
	a season - in autumn, winter, spring, summer
	in the expressions - in the morning/afternoon/evening
ON	**a day** - on Tuesday, on 2nd July, Christmas Day
	part of a day - on Saturday morning

Put *at, in* or *on* into these sentences:

1. Don't you love getting up late . . . . the weekend?

2. Our neighbours go on holiday . . . . spring.

3. I'd like to travel to Glasgow . . . . 3rd August.

4. I'll see you . . . . the morning.

5. I always go to town to do some shopping . . . . Saturday.

6. It can get cold here . . . . January so bring warm clothes!

7. George is often late . . . . Monday mornings and so is the boss.

8. The last bus goes . . . . midnight and taxis are very expensive.

9. It was nice to meet all my friends . . . . New Year.

10. We usually visit my wife's family . . . . New Year's Day.

11. I think Max was in London for the first time . . . . 1993.

12. Could you take your holiday . . . . September this year?

13. Susie has a lot of work to do . . . . the moment.

14. Would you like to go sailing . . . . Saturday afternoon?

15. The train leaves . . . . 8.45 . . . . the evening.

16. Would you like to go out for dinner . . . . your birthday?

17. We want to give Miranda a surprise party . . . . Friday.

8.7 Useful adverbs

Exercise 1

Complete each sentence with one of the following adverbs. Use each word once.

about	finally	normally	really
fast	hard	quite	slowly

1. Could you speak more . . . ., please? It's difficult for Yoshiko to understand.
2. Are you sure? Do you . . . . want to go away this weekend?
3. Freddy is . . . . tall but not as tall as me.
4. What's the time? - I think it's . . . . one o'clock, but I'm not sure.
5. Don't drive so . . . . ! We're in the centre of town!
6. Steve . . . . gets home about six, but tonight he's going to be a bit late.
7. After waiting for over an hour, we . . . . boarded the plane.
8. I know your exam is next week, but don't work too . . . .

Exercise 2

Now do the same with these adverbs:

carefully	nearly	quickly	usually
immediately	occasionally	unfortunately	well

1. Only a few more miles to go! We're . . . . home.
2. Help! Come . . . . ! I'm going to drop this!
3. I don't want to forget, so I'll do it . . . .
4. I love listening to Jeff play the piano. He plays so . . . .
5. Now watch . . . . I want you to do this in a minute.
6. We . . . . eat out, but not very often.
7. I'd love to come to your party but . . . . I'm out of the country that week.
8. I . . . . take sugar, but I can drink it without.

70

8.8 Adjective phrases

Exercise 1
Complete each sentence with one of the adjective phrases below. Use each phrase once only.

afraid of	full of	interested in	sure about
engaged to	good at	pleased with	worried about

1. My boss was . . . . my work and put up my salary.
2. What's Martin so . . . . ? - He's taking his driving test tomorrow!
3. Lynda is . . . . Brian. They're getting married next year.
4. I'm not very . . . . cooking but I do my best.
5. We know Paula is coming but we aren't . . . . Judy.
6. Your homework is . . . . mistakes! You must be more careful!
7. Cheryl looks bored. I don't think she's very . . . . ballet.
8. We got to the airport early because we were . . . . missing the plane.

Exercise 2

Now do the same with these phrases:

annoyed with	kind of	sorry for	terrified of
fond of	late for	terrible at	wrong with

1. It was very . . . . you to help me. - Not at all.
2. At school I was . . . . English. It was my worst subject.
3. Where's the bus? We're going to be . . . . work.
4. Susan stayed out all night. Her parents were very . . . . her.
5. Something's . . . . this photocopier. It won't work.
6. Harry is very . . . . his grandchildren. He'll do anything for them.
7. Damien is . . . . spiders and jumps every time he sees one.
8. I feel really . . . . Jeremy. He hasn't got any money and he's lost his job.

71

8.9 Verbs with at/to

Complete each sentence by using *at* or *to*.

1. Josie's plane gets . . . . New York at ten o'clock.

2. Susan, come and look . . . . these fish in the river.

3. We often go . . . . Macdonald's on Saturday.

4. Charlie comes . . . . work by helicopter every day.

5. People will laugh . . . . you if you wear that silly tie!

6. Susie writes . . . . her boyfriend every day!

7. Can we stop . . . . the supermarket on the way home?

8. I want to give this ring . . . . my favourite granddaughter.

9. Darren only listens . . . . pop music on the radio.

10. I want to talk . . . . you about something very serious.

11. Who does this book belong . . . . ? - I think it's Harry's.

12. We want to arrive . . . . the airport in good time.

13. Throw the ball . . . . the tin and try to knock it down.

14. Muriel prefers living in the town . . . . living in the country.

15. I can't lend my CD player . . . . everybody who asks me!

16. Could you explain this word . . . . me? I can't understand it.

17. What's everybody staring . . . . ? It's only a wasp!

18. Could you pass this note . . . . Miss Johnson?

Now underline the verb and the preposition. This will help you remember them.

8.10 Verbs with from/for/of/on

Exercise 1

Complete each sentence by using *from* or *for*:

1. I had no money so I had to borrow some . . . . Jim.

2. The thief stole Mabel's purse . . . . her handbag.

3. Which company do you work . . . . ?

4. Good morning. I'm the manager. What can I do . . . . you?

5. I'm looking . . . . my book. I left it somewhere in this room.

6. The two murderers escaped . . . . prison last night.

7. I'd like to thank you . . . . all your help.

8. Rupert should apologise . . . . being so late.

9. Right, so who is going to pay . . . . the drinks?

10. I'm Dutch. Which country do you come . . . . ?

11. You work too hard! You should ask your boss . . . . a holiday!

Exercise 2

Now complete these sentences by using *of* or *on*:

1. George spends all his money . . . . computer games.

2. Can you think . . . . a word that means the same as "unhappy"?

3. This food reminds me . . . . the time I went to Spain.

4. Are you going to play tennis? - It depends . . . . the weather.

5. It's so noisy in here! I can't concentrate . . . . my work!

Now underline the verb and preposition in each sentence so that you can remember them more easily.

8.11 Prepositional phrases

Exercise 1

Complete each sentence with one of the phrases below. Use each phrase once only.

at least	for ages	in a hurry	in private
by air	for example	in love	in time

1. Jo never travels . . . . as she hates flying.

2. Why does Nigel run everywhere? He's always . . . .

3. Luckily we arrived just . . . . to catch the last bus.

4. The organisers expect . . . . 70 people to come to the meeting but there could be many more.

5. Have you got any identification, ... a driving licence?

6. Oh, hello! I haven't seen you . . . . ! How are you?

7. Kevin keeps sending me flowers. I think he must be . . . . !

8. Can I speak to you . . . . ? I don't want the others to hear.

Exercise 2

Now do the same with these sentences:

out of work	in fact	on foot	on the phone
in his forties	on his own	on holiday	on time

1. We came back . . . . I'm sure the walk was good for us.

2. The plane left . . . . but it arrived an hour late.

3. After the children left, Joe lived . . . . for a few years.

4. I think my boss is . . . . but it's difficult to say exactly how old he is.

5. Ruth is away . . . . at a hotel somewhere in the Bahamas.

6. Is that boy still . . . . ? Who is he talking to now?

7. If the factory closes, 150 people will be . . . .

8. People think he comes from the USA but . . . . he's Canadian.

8.12 Link words

In these exercises you will see words like *and, but* and *as soon as*, which you can use to join two parts of a sentence together.

Exercise 1

Match the two halves of the sentences. Use each half once only. Write your answers in the boxes.

1. The weather was terrible
2. I'm taking my car
3. Frank didn't go to bed
4. I'll phone you
5. The phone stopped ringing
6. Sally went to bed early
7. My father was very angry

a. when he saw the mess.
b. as soon as I have any news.
c. and John is taking his.
d. before I could answer it.
e. although he was very tired.
f. so we didn't go out.
g. because she was so tired.

1	
2	
3	
4	
5	
6	
7	

Exercise 2

Now do the same with these sentence halves:

1. We're going on holiday to the place
2. You must speak slowly and clearly
3. Maggie drives much more carefully
4. The team played very well
5. I met an old friend
6. Angela usually has a shower every morning
7. We can't start this meeting

a. so that your students can understand.
b. than her husband does.
c. while I was doing some shopping.
d. until everyone is here.
e. where we first met.
f. but they didn't play well enough to win the match.
g. after she has breakfast.

1	
2	
3	
4	
5	
6	
7	

Now underline all the link words. Write sentences using them.

8.13 One word – two uses

Some words can be both a noun and a verb. The word *walk* is a good example:

Why don't you walk to the station. It isn't far. > *walk* is a verb here.

Let's go for a walk. It's a lovely afternoon. > *walk* is a noun here.

Here are some words which can be a verb or a noun. Use each word to complete the pairs of sentences.

answer	dream	drive	help	phone
plan	promise	queue	rain	visit

1. a. Every night I . . . . about the girl I met on holiday.

   b. Cathy had a horrible . . . . about falling out of a plane.

2. a. We had to . . . . for hours to get tickets for the concert.

   b. There was already a long . . . . when we got to the theatre.

3. a. Trudy's gone to Manchester to . . . . her grandparents.

   b. Mike's away on a . . . . to his uncle in Madrid.

4. a. I'll give you my home number so you can . . . . me there.

   b. Is Mandy still on the . . . . ? I've got a call to make!

5. a. Could you . . . . me to carry these boxes to the car?

   b. Do you need any . . . . with the washing-up?

6. a. Look at those clouds! I'm sure it's going to . . . .

   b. The . . . . came down so heavily that we had to go inside.

7. a. June didn't learn to . . . . a car until she was thirty.

   b. Let's go for a . . . . in the country this afternoon.

8. a. Don't just live for today. You must . . . . for the future.

   b. The . . . . of the hotel will show you where the pool is.

9. a. You will come, won't you? - Yes, I will. I . . . .

   b. Hamish didn't come. He didn't keep his . . . .

10. a. . . . . my question! Who was that girl you were with?

    b. Jim wrote the company a letter but he never got an . . . .

76

Chapter Nine

Word Puzzles

1. **Enjoy your English.**

   If you don't enjoy learning, you won't learn. If you find something boring, stop doing it! You will learn best when you are interested and involved.

2. **If you enjoy word puzzles, try to find more.**

   All word puzzles teach vocabulary. The more you do, the more words you will learn.

9.1 Verb snake

Complete the snake by using one of these verbs in the sentences. The first letter of each verb is the same as the last letter of the verb in the sentence before.

draw	know	lend	phone	stop	travel
drop	laugh	need	pull	tell	wait
help	learn	pass	put	thank	want

1. How can I make this room more fun to live in? -
    . . . . some posters up!

2. We want to . . . . you for all your help.

3. What's the time? - I'm afraid I don't . . . .

4. I usually . . . . for the bus outside the post office.

5. Sally hopes to . . . . around America one day.

6. I don't think that programme is funny. Other people
    . . . . at it but not me!

7. Can you . . . . me to move this, please. I can't do
    it by myself.

8. If you push the table, I'll . . . . it.

9. Ivor would like to . . . . another language.

10. Do you . . . . some more water to wash the
    window?

11. Could you . . . . me a map to show me the way to
    your house?

12. I don't . . . . to go to bed! I'm not tired!

13. Could you . . . . me the time? - Yes, it's ten
    o'clock.

14. Could you . . . . me your pen? Mine doesn't work.

15. Be careful with those glasses! Don't . . . . them!

16. Could you . . . . me the salt, please?

17. Please . . . . talking. I'm trying to think.

18. I want to . . . . James. What's his number?

9.2 Odd one out

Which of the four words is different, and why? If it's difficult to explain why, choose from the list at the bottom of the page.

The others:

1.	aunt	daughter	mother	(nephew)	*are women/female*
2.	bathroom	bedroom	garden	kitchen	. . . .
3.	beer	cake	coffee	tea	. . . .
4.	twelve	sixty	twice	sixteen	. . . .
5.	eyes	knee	mouth	nose,	. . . .
6.	Ecuador	German	Spain	Zambia	. . . .
7.	drums	goal	guitar	piano	. . . .
8.	bicycle	bus	car	lorry	. . . .
9.	football	hockey	judo	photography	. . . .
10.	autumn	summer	weekend	winter	. . . .
11.	breakfast	dinner	lemon	lunch	. . . .
12.	afternoon	evening	journey	morning	. . . .
13.	cup	glass	mug	plate	. . . .
14.	bird	cat	dog	horse	. . . .
15.	rain	snow	spring	wind	. . . .
16.	cigar	cigarette	pipe	ice-cream	. . . .
17.	forest	lake	river	sea	. . . .
18.	cooker	fridge	grill	shower	. . . .
19.	boots	gloves	shoes	slippers	. . . .
20.	book	film	magazine	newspaper	. . . .

The others

a. can't fly   b. have four wheels   c. are countries   d. are in the kitchen

e. are inside a house   f. are meals   g. are musical instruments   h. are numbers

i. are on the face   j. are parts of the day   k. are seasons   l. are sports

m. are types of weather   n. are water   o. are women/female

p. are things you drink   q. are things you read   r. are things you smoke

s. are things you use to drink   t. are things you wear on your feet

9.3 Verb square – 1

Look in the word square and find the past form of the verbs below:

break	forget	lend	run	stop	think
cut	hide	make	shut	swim	try
fall	is	meet	sleep	take	wear
find	leave	put	spend	tell	win

The words can go across or down, or diagonally left to right. The same letter may be in more than one word.

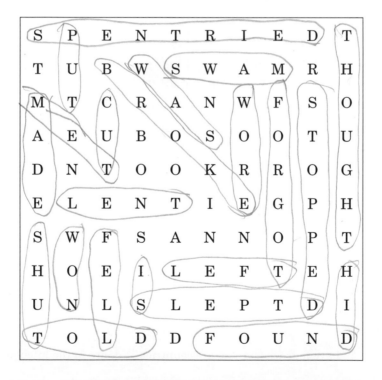

Remember to check if the past form is irregular when you learn a new verb. Remember also that some verbs that end in -ed in their past form have changes in their spelling, for example:

cry   cried   permit   permitted

A good dictionary should show you these spelling changes.

9.4 Verb square – 2

Look in the word square and find the past tense of these verbs:

begin	do	feel	have	read	see
buy	drink	get	hear	ride	sing
can	drive	give	know	ring	sit
come	eat	go	pay	say	write

The words can go across or down or diagonally left to right. The same letter may be in more than one word.

Remember there are only about 100 important irregular verbs, but these are some of the most common words in English.

9.5 Crossword – 1

Complete these sentences to complete the crossword puzzle on the opposite page. You will see the words you need at the bottom of the next page but try to do the puzzle without looking at them.

ACROSS

1. Sally's father was so . . . . when she crashed his car!
3. I'm very . . . . Shall we have something to drink?
5. It was . . . . to see so many of my old friends again.
6. Smoking is . . . ., but a lot of people smoke anyway.
8. It's getting . . . . in here. Could you switch the light on?
9. There's some really . . . . countryside in this part of the world.
11. Let's leave as early as . . . . in the morning.
13. Mark's quite tall, with . . . . hair and brown eyes.
15. . . . . New Year!
16. I've just washed this shirt but it's still . . . .
17. I'm not really . . . . in reading. I prefer sport.
20. There are more people here than we expected. I'll get some . . . . chairs.
21. Are you . . . . on Monday? We're all going bowling.
22. This dress is too . . . . for me. Have you got a smaller size?
23. We live in a very . . . . part of town.
24. It's . . . . to explain what the problem is, but I'll try.

DOWN

1. Do you know where Bill is? - No, I'm . . . . not.
2. Let's go for a walk. - . . . . idea!
3. There's been a . . . . accident! Three people are dead.
4. This dictionary is much more . . . . than my old one.
7. We always go to a disco. Let's go somewhere . . . . for a change.
10. Carol is so . . . . She leaves her things all over the floor!
12. We must speak to Mrs Parker at once. It's very . . . .

82

14. It was very cold last night so the roads are . . . . this morning.
15. The coffee's too . . . . so I'll leave it for a minute.
18. I'm . . . . I had a late night last night.
19. Isn't Canberra the capital of Australia? - Yes, that's . . . .

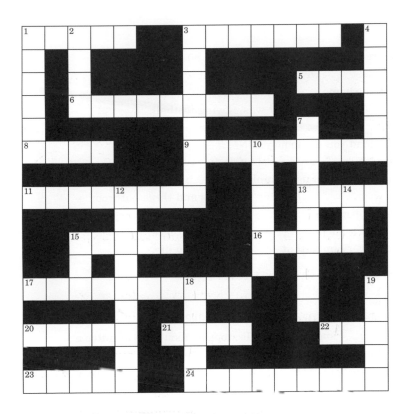

afraid, angry, beautiful, big, dangerous, dark, different, difficult, dirty, extra, fair, free, good, happy, hot, icy, important, interested, nice, possible, quiet, right, terrible, thirsty, tired, untidy, useful

9.6 Crossword – 2

Complete these sentences to complete the crossword puzzle on the opposite page. You will see the words you need at the bottom of the next page, but try to do the puzzle without looking at them.

ACROSS

1. Have you read "......... the World in 80 Days"?
4. There's .... wrong with the car. It won't start.
8. What was the game ....? - Not bad.
9. I hurt .... leg while I was playing football.
10. Please sit .... Can I get you something to drink?
12. Did Mary lend you the money? - No, ... didn't.
14. The train leaves .... six o'clock.
16. Is Brian coming with us? I think ....
18. Their new .... has five bedrooms and three bathrooms.
21. What does 'terrified' ....? - Very frightened.
22. Do you know who .... girls are over there?
24. 1994 was a very important .... in my life.
25. I've got so much to .... this week.
26. More tea? - .... please.
28. Can I come in? - Of .... you can.
29. A coffee, please. - With or .... milk?
34. Is it .... snowing? - No. It stopped about five minutes ago.
36. My alarm didn't ring so I got .... late.
37. I waited .... that bus for half an hour yesterday!
38. Who wants the .... piece of cake?
40. How .... is Pat? - In her thirties, I think.
41. How long does it .... you to get to work? - About an hour.
42. Are you sure you .... want to be a soldier?
43. Would you like .... biscuit? - No, thanks. One is enough.

DOWN

1. We played .... a team which was much better than ours.
2. The tickets are very cheap. They're .... a pound.
3. What .... Joe do in his spare time? - As little as possible!
4. Oh no! That woman's wearing the .... dress as I am!
5. The film was so bad that we left before the ....
6. .... are you? - Fine, thanks. And you?
7. Exactly how many cars has your boss ....? - At least six.
11. So you speak English. What .... languages do you know?

84

13. I'll tell you . . . . soon as I can.
15. What's . . . . matter? - I've got a headache.
16. He . . . . he loves me but does he really mean it?
17. Which coat is yours? - The dark blue . . . .
19. Put your bag . . . . the seat. It should be safe there.
20. The Smiths went . . . . Germany for their holiday.
21. . . . . I borrow your dictionary?
23. It was . . . . a nice day that we decided to go for a walk.
27. Some . . . . spend lots of money on clothes but Bill doesn't.
28. Have you got any . . . . ? - Yes, two boys.
29. The . . . . gets smaller every year.
30. Could you come . . . . .way, please?
31. Don't forget to switch the computer . . . .
32. It takes about five minutes to drive . . . . the tunnel.
33. Now I live in London, but I . . . . to live in New York.
35. My Spanish is good but I only speak a . . . . Italian.
39. This exercise is more difficult . . . . the other one.

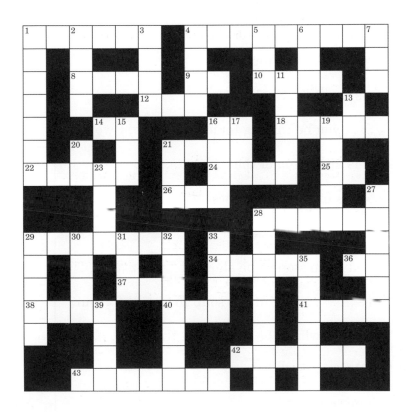

against, another, around, as, at, children, course, do, does, down, end, for, got, house, how, last, like, little, may, mean, my, off, old, one, only, other, people, really, same, says, she, so, something, still, such, take, than, the, this, those, through, to, under, up, used, without, world, year, yes

9.7 Word ladder

Change the top word into the word at the bottom. Each time you must change one letter only in the word before. If you don't know the word, guess what is possible and check in your dictionary. Guessing and using a good dictionary are two important ways to help you to improve your English.

1. Go on foot.	**WALK**
2. I want to . . . . to you about something.	
3. Not short.	
4. There's a big . . . . around the house.	
5. Don't climb that tree. You might	
6. Your glass is empty. Shall I . . . . it?	
7. . . . . you be coming tomorrow? - No, I won't.	
8. The shop is at the top of the	
9. The match is in the gymnastics	
10. I'll be back in . . . . an hour.	
11. He wanted us to stop so he shouted ". . . . . !"	
12. Put more . . . . in the soup to give it flavour.	
13. Don't buy it now! It'll be cheaper in the	
14. Not female.	
15. 1.61 kilometres	**MILE**

Test 1

Choose the best alternative to complete each sentence.

1. We . . . . TV for most of the evening.
   a. looked   b. looked for   c. saw   d. watched

2. We'll have to use the stairs. The lift is . . . . order.
   a. in   b. out of   c. outside   d. without

3. You'll feel much better, if you . . . . smoking.
   a. get on   b. get out   c. give in   d. give up

4. We were stuck in a traffic . . . . for over an hour.
   a. jam   b. light   c. line   d. stop

5. Flight 547 to Manchester is now ready for . . . .
   a. boarding   b. entering   c. flying   d. leaving

6. Who's going to help me . . . . the balloons for the party?
   a. blow down   b. blow up   c. get down   d. get up

7. Steve plays the . . . . in a pop group.
   a. concert   b. drums   c. opera   d. tunes

8. This is the biggest football . . . . in the country.
   a. court   b. gym   c. ring   d. stadium

9. There will be . . . . rain during the night.
   a. big   b. great   c. heavy   d. long

10. What would you like to drink? - A . . . . , , ... water, please.
    a. cup   b. bottle   c. glass   d. mineral

11. My aunt and . . . . , , . . have been married for 20 years now.
    a. boyfriend   b. husband   c. grandson   d. uncle

12. We asked the . . . . at the hotel to get us a taxi.
    a. lawyer   b. receptionist   c. reporter   d. stewardess

13. Sandra was never very good . . . . geography.
    a. at   b. for   c. of   d. to

14. What's your favourite . . . . ? - Physics.
    a. break   b. study   c. studying   d. subject

15. I don't need as many as twenty. Just give me . . . .
    a. a dozen   b. a hundred   c. thirty   d. zero

Test 2

Choose the best alternative to complete each sentence.

1. What's the time now? - It's . . . . *at* . . . . twelve o'clock.
    a. at   b. near   c. nearly   d. most

2. Did you hear the news . . . . . . *on* . . . . the radio?
    a. at   b. by   c. in   d. on

3. Surely Pete can't do all that work . . . . . *by* . . . . his own!
    a. by   b. for   c. on   d. with

4. Sally's got an office . . . . . . *on* . . . . the fifth floor.
    a. at   b. by   c. in   d. on

5. I'm going to the . *optician's* . . . to get my new glasses.
    a. artist's   b. engineer's   c. mechanic's   d. optician's

6. Excuse me, are you the . . . . *owner* . . . . of this bicycle?
    a. customer   b. driver   c. manager   d. owner

7. Could you . . . . a picture of us with my camera?
    a. do   b. give   c. make   d. take

8. I'd like to book two . . . . rooms and one double, please.
    a. alone   b. only   c. single   d. singular

9. Call a . . . . There's water coming through the ceiling.
    a. nurse   b. plumber   c. priest   d. sailor

10. My dog was very ill so I took him to a . . . .
    a. dentist   b. engineer   c. mechanic   d. vet

11. It wasn't very far so we decided to go . . . . foot.
    a. at   b. on   c. to   d. with

12. The Smiths got the car . . . . from Dover to Calais.
    a. ferry   b. journey   c. travel   d. voyage

13. Why don't people put their rubbish in the litter . . . . ?
    a. bins   b. booths   c. stops   d. vans

14. Can I borrow your . . . . to cut my nails?
    a. comb   b. razor   c. knives   d. scissors

15. I hired a . . . . so that I could film the wedding.
    a. camcorder   b. cassette recorder   c. record   d. system

Test 3

Choose the best alternative to complete each sentence.

1. The sea conditions are just right for us to go . . . .
   a. cycling   b. skating   c. climbing   d. surfing

2. It's cold outside. Don't forget to take your . . . .
   a. pants   b. scarf   c. shorts   d. suit

3. Try the . . . . trout. It's usually very good.
   a. grilled   b. mashed   c. roast   d. minced

4. That rump . . . . was delicious!
   a. mousse   b. salad   c. steak   d. sole

5. Here's a . . . . for you to put your coat on.
   a. collector   b. cupboard   c. exhibition   d. hanger

6. My driving . . . . said that I was certain to pass my test.
   a. director   b. inspector   c. instructor   d. manager

7. The . . . . of the shop gave me my money back.
   a. host   b. manager   c. operator   d. runner

8. Who was the . . . . of this piece of music?
   a. composer   b. composition   c. translator   d. reporter

9. The word '. . . . .' does not rhyme with the others.
   a. clear   b. wear   c. hear   d. dear

10. That's the friend . . . . car I borrowed.
    a. he's   b. whose   c. who's   d. his

11. It was a very serious illness and Max still feels very . . . .
    a. fair   b. faulty   c. soft   d. weak

12. Business people usually . . . . hands when they first meet.
    a. have   b. shake   c. lock   d. hold

13. Let's . . . . the bell and see if she's in.
    a. knock   b. listen to   c. play   d. ring

14. I've . . . . my mind. I think I'll stay at home this evening.
    a. changed   b. done   c. made   d. thought

15. Can we stop for a minute? These suitcases are very . . . .
    a. careful   b. empty   c. heavy   d. tired

89

Test 4

Choose the best alternative to complete each sentence.

1. You look tired. Why don't you have a . . . . ?
   a. lie   b. rest   c. stay   d. stop

2. . . . . care when you bring that dish. It's hot.
   a. Be   b. Have   c. Make   d. Take

3. Kyoko soon made . . . . with the other people in the class.
   a. friend   b. friends   c. friendly   d. friendship

4. You need a . . . . personality to do well in this job.
   a. high   b. weak   c. strong   d. thick

5. The fog was so . . . . that we couldn't see where
   we were going.
   a. big   b. great   c. strong   d. thick

6. The policeman asked to see my . . . . licence.
   a. drive   b. auto   c. driver   d. driving

7. You must show your . . . . card if you want to get in.
   a. identical   b. identify   c. identifying   d. identity

8. The weather . . . . said it would be sunny on Saturday.
   a. forecast   b. news   c. record   d. story

9. Could you pass me the butter? - Certainly. Here . . . .
   a. are you   b. you are   c. is it   d. there is

10. Sorry I'm late. – That's all right. It . . . .
    a. doesn't matter   b. doesn't miss   c. does nothing   d. goes well

11. How much bread do we need? - Just a small . . . .
    a. bake   b. cook   c. loaf   d. stuff

12. And what would you like for the . . . . course, sir?
    a. big   b. great   c. main   d. principal

13. . . . . the third on the right, just after the bank.
    a. Get   b. Go   c. Take   d. Turn

14. Have you got . . . . ? - I'm afraid not. I don't smoke.
    a. fire   b. a fire   c. lighter   d. a light

15. Our plane should . . . . in about half an hour.
    a. go up   b. lend   c. put up   d. take off

Test 5

Choose the best alternative to complete each sentence.

1. Turn right . . . . the traffic lights and you'll see the cinema.
   a. at   b. off   c. on   d. over

2. I rented a house . . . . Suffolk Avenue.
   a. among   b. between   c. in   d. through

3. Did you do anything special . . . . the weekend?
   a. at   b. in   c. on   d. to

4. Could you meet me . . . . Friday afternoon?
   a. at   b. in   c. on   d. to

5. I . . . . have toast but I wasn't very hungry this morning.
   a. nearly   b. normally   c. quite   d. well

6. This letter is full . . . . mistakes. Could you do it again, please.
   a. from   b. in   c. of   d. with

7. Tricia is really fond . . . . Andy. Did you see the present he gave her?
   a. for   b. of   c. on   d. with

8. Pat's still . . . . the phone. Who is she talking to?
   a. in   b. on   c. over   d. to

9. Charles has been out of . . . . for over a year now.
   a. employ   b. employed   c. job   d. work

10. I'll call you . . . . I have any news.
    a. as soon   b. as soon as   c. soonest   d. while

11. I'm very . . . . Is there anything cool to drink?
    a. dirty   b. hunger   c. hungry   d. thirsty

12. Can you come to the meeting? - No, I'm . . . . not.
    a. afraid   b. sorry   c. sure   d. think

13. Joe's not really very . . . . in the theatre. He prefers the cinema.
    a. excited   b. interested   c. fond   d. keen

14. It . . . . me about an hour to get to work.
    a. gets   b. makes   c. spends   d. takes

15 What's the . . . .? – I can't find my wallet.
   a. halt   b. matter   c. stop   d. wrong

Answers

1.2 1.c 2.b 3.f 4.g 5.i 6.e 7.a 8.h 9.d

1.3 catch, fare

1.4 1.speak English, 2.do your homework, 3.have a bath, 4.make a mistake, 5.play golf, 6.ride a bike, 7.catch a bus, 8.watch TV 9.catch a bus 10.speak English 11.play golf 12.watch TV

1.5 1.friendly 2.swimming 3.dangerous 4.painting 5.information 6.windy

1.6 1.one, brother, come, front, love, money 2.hot, copy, job, long, often, stop 3.go, close, home, most, open, show

1.7 1.hurry 2.delicious 3.artist 4.of course 5.give up 6.department store 7.terrible 8.out of order 9.recommend 10.shampoo

1.8 1.traffic, passport, flight, travel 2.leave, take, miss, board 3.in, through, from 4.at, in, for 5.man, hair, glasses 6.up, up, up 7.Can, down, like

1.9 1.tall and thin 2.thin and bald 3.tired and sleepy 4.old and poor 5.nice and tasty 6.short and fat 7.young and happy 8.tired and dirty 9.wet and windy 10. rich and famous 11.nice and sunny 12.hot and angry

2.1 1.furniture: armchair, bed, chair, sofa, stool, table 2.family: brother-in-law, cousin, grandson, nephew, parents, uncle 3.colours: black, blue, green, red, white, yellow 4.music: concert, drums, opera singer, play a tune, pop song, violin

2.2 1.sport: baseball team, football stadium, play volleyball, referee, tennis court, win the match 2.drinks: bottle of wine, cup of coffee, glass of milk, lemonade, mineral water, orange juice 3.clothes: blouse, long skirt, pair of socks, pair of trousers, smart suit, warm coat 4.weather: heavy rain, temperature, shower, sunny, sunshine, windy

2.3 **Days**: 1.Monday 2.Tuesday 3.Wednesday 4.Thursday 5.Friday 6.Saturday 7.Sunday **Parts of a day**: 1.morning 2.afternoon 3.evening 4.night **Months**: 1.January 2.February 3.March 4.April 5.May 6.June 7.July 8.August 9.September 10.October 1.November 12.December **Seasons**: 1.spring 2.summer 3.autumn 4.winter **Time:** 1.second 2.minute 3.hour 4.day 5.week 6.month 7.year

2.4 **Men**: husband, uncle, prince, nephew, boyfriend, grandfather, king, grandson **Women**: wife, grandmother, granddaughter, aunt, princess, niece, widow, queen, girlfriend **Both**: teacher, violinist, detective, lawyer, receptionist, manager, tourist, dancer, reporter, pilot, artist, engineer, mechanic

2.5 **Subjects:** geography, mathematics, physics **Things:** desk, dictionary, ruler **Places:** primary school, secondary school **People:** headmistress, schoolteacher, student **Verbs:** take, translate **Other:** good/bad at, lunch break

3.1 **Exercise 1** 1.19 2.18 3.87 4.11 5.54 6.43 7.14 8.100 9.12 10.98 11.1.5 12.17 13.76 14.65 15.32 16.1,000 17.21 18.2$^{1}/_{2}$ 19.212 20.0 21.3,679 22.1,300,010 **Exercise 2** 1.first 2.second 3.third 4.fourth 5.fifth 6.eighth 7.ninth 8.twelfth 9.fifteenth 10.twentieth 11.twenty-third 12.twenty-seventh 13.thirtieth 14.thirty-first

3.2 **Exercise 1** 1.1969, nineteen sixty-nine 2.1789, seventeen eighty-nine 3.1945, nineteen forty-five 4.1989, nineteen eighty-nine **Exercise 2** 1.the first of January 2.February the twenty-ninth 3.the fourth of July 4.December the twenty-fourth

3.3 1.nine o'clock 2.six thrty 3.(a) quarter to seven 4.two ten 5.eleven fifty 6.three fifteen 7.twenty-five past one 8.five to one 9.five thirty-five 10.nearly quarter past four 11.just after seven forty 12.almost five past three

3.4 **Exercise 1** 1.f 2.a 3.h 4.g 5.i 6.d 7.b 8.c **Exercise 2** 1.i 2.c 3.a 4.b 5.g 6.d 7.f 8.h

3.5 1.b 2.d 3.a 4.b 5.d 6.b 7.d 8.a 9.a 10.a 11.b 12.c 13.c 14.a

3.6 1.cowboy 2.guitar 3.violin 4.referee 5.stadium 6.shorts 7.penalty 8.lose 9.take 10.camera 11.video 12.horror

3.7 1.receptionist 2.single room 3.caravan 4.bike 5.airport 6.train 7.restaurant 8.disco 9.yacht 10.swimming 11.pool 12.credit card 13.guide book 14.suitcase 15.aspirin

3.8 1.doctor 2.nurse 3.pilot 4.cook 5.teacher 6.sailor 7.priest 8.vet 9.footballer 10.waiter 11.librarian 12.taxi driver 13.car mechanic 14.hairdresser 15.office worker 16.lorry driver 17.shop assistant 18.tourist guide 19.plumber 20.factory worker

3.9 1.We flew. 2.We went by bus. 3.We took a taxi. 4.We came by train. 5.We hired a car. 6.We came on foot. 7.We got the car ferry. 8.We came on our bikes. 9.We took the underground. 1.by plane 2.coaches 3.by boat 4.walk 5.cycle

3.10 1.I got up at 7.30. 2.I had a shower. 3.I waited for the bus. 4.I had a meeting at 9. 5.I went to the dentist. 6.I met Mark for lunch. 7.I was busy all afternoon. 8.We had dinner. 9.We kissed goodnight. After have: have a shower, have a meeting, have dinner. The following can follow have: a sandwich, a headache, a good time, a coffee, a problem, an idea, a bad throat, a beer.

3.11 1.bike 2.crossing 3.bus stop 4.road sign 5.lorry 6.van 7.litter bin 8.pavement 9.policeman 10.traffic lights 11.public toilet (loo) 12.phone box 13.motorbike 14.lamp post 15.pram

3.12 1.clock 2.pen 3.key 4.wallet 5.credit card 6.calculator 7.toothbrush 8.glasses 9.pencil 10.watch 11.comb 12.notes 13.cheque 14.file 15.contact lenses 16.coins 17.magazine 18.scissors 19.envelope 20.stamp

3.13 1.mobile phone 2.headphones 3.radio/cassette recorder 4.car stereo 5.camera 6.camcorder 7.personal CD 8.personal stereo 9.stereo system

3.14 1.apple 2. cherries 3. pineapple 4 orange 5. lemon 6. grapes 7. pear 8.peach 9.banana 10.peas 11.cabbage 12.potatoes 13.carrot 14.beans 15.onions 16.lettuce 17.cucumber 18.tomatoes

3.15 1.football 2.tennis 3.golf 4.skiing 5.skating 6.cycling 7.fishing 8.sailing 9.windsurfing 10.swimming 11.table tennis 12.surfing 13.riding 14.basketball 15.American football

3.16 1.shirt 2.shoe 3.socks 4.trainers 5.dress 6.skirt 7.bra 8.tights 9.anorak 10.coat 11.jacket 12.track-suit 13.jeans 14.scarf 15.suit 16.trousers 17.cap 18.T-shirt 19.boots 20.shorts 21.jumper/sweater/pullover 22.hat 23.knickers/pants 24.underpants

3.17 **Starters:** vegetable soup, fruit juice **Fish/shellfish:** lobster, grilled trout, Scottish salmon, sole **Meat:** lamb cutlets, rump steak, roast chicken, roast pork **Vegetables:** cauliflower, peas, beans, carrots **Potatoes:** roast potatoes, baked potato, mashed potato, French fries **Desserts:** ice cream, chocolate mousse, apple pie, yoghurt, fruit salad

4.1 1.careful 2.sunny 3.surprised 4.surprising 5.funny 6.worried 7.stormy 8.married 9.interesting 10.wonderful 11.beautiful 12.sleepy 13.useful 14.embarrassed 15.tiring 16.excited

4.2 1.cooker 2.building 3.information 4.meaning 5.recorder 6.beginning 7.shopping 8.exhibition 9.hanger 10.smoking 11.maker 12.direction 13.meeting 14.translation 15.freezer 16.heating 17.collection 18.painting

4.3 1.actor 2.baker 3.collector 4.director 5.driver 6.farmer 7.gardener 8.inspector 9.instructor 10.manager 11.operator 12.player 13.reporter 14.rider 15.runner 16.sailor 17.teacher 18.translator 19.visitor 20.worker 1.driver 2.manager 3.collector 4.reporter 5.player/manager 6.instructor

4.4 **-an:** Brazilian, Canada, German, Hungary, Mexican, Russia   **-ish:** Finnish, Ireland, Polish, Scotland, Spanish, Turkey   **-ese:** Chinese, Japan, Lebanese, Portugal, Taiwanese, Vietnam   **others:** French, Greece, Omani, Switzerland, Thai, Wales

4.5 1.flying 2.daily 3.illness 4.anger 5.composer 6.faulty 7.politician 8.stormy 9.possibilities 10.shorten 11.healthy 12.hearing

5.1 1.shop, top, want, what 2.boot, new, two, you 3.chair, their, wear, where 4.make, rain, steak, they 5.cheer, dear, here, near 6. know, phone, toast, toe

5.2 1.a.too b.two 2.a.son b.sun 3.a.sea b.see 4.a.it's b.its 5.a.buy b.by 6.a.hear b.here 7.a.right b.write 8.a.who's b.whose

5.3 1.a.passed b.past 2.a.knew b.new 3.a.their b.there 4.a.hour b.our 5.a.wood b.would 6.a.meat b.meet 7.a.weak b.week 8.a.some b.sum 9.a.there b.they're 10.a.fair b.fare 11.a.pair b.pear 12.a.wait b.weight

5.4 1.shall 2.own 3.well 4.move 5.cow 6.phone 7.coat 8.pear 9.here 10.cost 11.after 12.eat 13.shout 14.tea 15.no 16.warm 17.said 18.white

5.5 1.April, breakfast, easy, husband, sweater, traffic 2.again, begin, between, enjoy, hotel, Japan 3.certainly, difficult, holiday, hospital, manager, telephone 4.another, banana, December, eleven, example, musician

6.1 **Exercise 1** 1.d 2.f 3.e 4.b 5.a 6.c 7.h 8.g   **Exercise 2** 1.e 2.a 3.g 4.h 5.d 6.c 7.b 8.f 1.shake hands 2.wear glasses 3.post a letter 4.improve your English

6.2 **Exercise 1** 1.a 2.e 3.d 4.c 5.g 6.h 7.b 8.f **Exercise 2** 1.c 2.b 3.e 4.d 5.g 6.h 7.f 8.a 1.sunny day 2.comfortable chair 3.long time 4.silly mistake

6.3 **Exercise 1** 1.read 2.eat 3.paint 4.ride 5.write 6.smile 7.dance 8.miss 9.drink 10.throw 11.open 12.walk **Exercise 2** 1.open 2.paint 3.eat 4.read 5.throw 6.ride 7.write/read 8.miss

6.4 **Exercise 1** 1.drive 2.sing 3.wash 4.cut 5.draw 6.fall 7.close 8.jump 9.kick 10.run 11.climb 12.cry **Exercise 2** 1.wash 2.sing 3.drive 4.draw 5.kick 6.climb 7.cut 8.close

6.5 1.shower 2.rest 3.cold 4.idea 5.difficulty 6.mistake 7.noise 8.cake 9.friends 10.call 11.time 12.seat 13.picture 14.taxi 15.care

6.6 1.beautiful 2.long 3.cold 4.strong 5.thick 6.high 7.funny 8.big 9.old 10.great

6.7 1.d 2.h 3.g 4.j 5.f 6.b 7.i 8.m 9.o 10.k 11.c 12.a 13.l 14.e 15.n 1.summer holiday 2.ice cream 3.weather forecast 4.ground floor

7.1 1.Yes I am. Can I help you? 2.Nothing special. Why? 3.Thank you. The same to you. 4. Certainly, here you are. 5. That's all right. It doesn't matter. 6.Thank you. It's nice to be here. 7.Oh no! What shall we do? 8.She doesn't feel very well.

7.2 1.g 2.e 3.h 4.f 5.j 6.i 7.d 8.c 9.a 10.b

7.3 **Conversation 1** 1.Are you ready 2.What would you like 3.soup of the day 4.for me, too 5.I'd like
Conversation 2 1.I'm very sorry 2.What a pity 3.How would you like it 4.something to drink 5.Thank you very much

7.4 **Conversation 1** 1.Excuse me 2.Could you tell me the way 3.Pardon 4.I'm afraid not 5.Why don't you ask 6.Good idea   **Conversation 2** 1.how to get to 2.of course 3.turn left 4.the second on the right 5.just after a supermarket 6.You're welcome

7.5 **Exercise 1** 1.h 2.g 3.f 4.e 5.b 6.c 7.a 8.d
Exercise 2 1.g 2.f 3.a 4.b 5.h 6.e 7.c 8.d

8.1 **Exercise 1** 1.babies 2.boxes 3.boys 4.children 5.classes 6.days 7.factories 8.knives 9.leaves 10.lunches 11.men 12.tomatoes 13.teeth 14.women
Exercise 2 1.strawberries 2.lorries 3.buses 4.sandwiches 5.ladies, gentlemen 6.feet

8.2 1.disagree 2.answer 3.lend 4.open 5.go up 6.lose 7.start 8.love 9.take off 10.cry 11.arrive 12.forget 13.buy 14.put on 15.finish/start 16.close/open 17.borrow/lend 18.hate/love 19.find/lose 20.leave/arrive 21.remember/forget 22.sell/buy 23.laugh/cry 24.ask/answer 25.come down/go up 26.take off/put on 27.land/take off 28.agree/disagree

8.3 1.difficult 2.cold 3.new 4.young 5.expensive 6.bad 7.first 8.long 9.tall 10.fast 11.open 12.late 13.big 14.high 15.left 16.wrong 17.cheap 18.wrong 19.hot 20.small 21.easy 22.slow 23.open 24.first

8.4 1.on 2.at 3.under 4.behind 5.in 6.through 7.down 8.over 9.outside 10.beside 11.between 12.near

8.5 1.a 2.c 3.b 4.c 5.a 6.b 7.c 8.c 9.b 10.b 11.c 12.b 13.d 14.d 15.b

8.6 1.at 2.in 3.on 4.in 5.on 6.in 7.on 8.at 9.at 10.on 11.in 12.in 13.at 14.on 15.at, in 16.on 17.on

8.7 **Exercise 1** 1.slowly 2.really 3.quite 4.about 5.fast 6.normally 7.finally 8.hard
Exercise 2 1.nearly 2.quickly 3.immediately 4.well 5.carefully 6.occasionally 7.unfortunately 8.usually

8.8 **Exercise 1** 1.pleased with 2.worried about 3.engaged to 4.good at 5.sure about 6.full of 7.interested in 8.afraid of   **Exercise 2** 1.kind of 2.terrible at 3.late for 4.annoyed with 5.wrong with 6.fond of 7.terrified of 8.sorry for

8.9 1.to 2.at 3.to 4.to 5.at 6.to 7.at 8.to 9.to 10.to 11.to 12.at 13.at 14.to 15.to 16.to 17.at 18.to

8.10 **Exercise 1**   1.from 2.from 3.for 4.for 5.for 6.from 7.for 8 for 9.for 10.from 11.for
Exercise 2 1.on 2.of 3.of 4.on 5.on

8.11 **Exercise 1**   1.by air 2.in a hurry 3.in time 4.at least 5.for example 6.for ages 7.in love 8.in private   **Exercise 2**   1.on foot 2.on time 3.on his own 4.in his forties 5.on holiday 6.on the phone 7.out of work 8.in fact

8.12 **Exercise 1**   1.f 2.c 3.e 4.b 5.d 6.g 7.a   **Exercise 2** 1.e 2.a 3.b 4.f 5.c 6.g 7.d

8.13 1.dream 2.queue 3.visit 4.phone 5.help 6.rain 7.drive 8.plan 9.promise 10.answer

9.1 1.put 2.thank 3.know 4.wait 5.travel 6.laugh 7.help 8.pull 9.learn 10.need 11.draw 12.want 13.tell 14.lend 15.drop 16.pass 17.stop 18.phone

9.2 1.nephew, o 2.garden, e 3.cake, p 4.twice, h 5.knee, i 6.German, c 7.goal, g 8.bicycle, b 9.photography l 10.weekend, k 11.lemon, f 12.journey, j 13.plate, s 14.bird, a 15.spring, m 16.ice-cream, r 17.forest, n 18.shower, d 19.gloves, t 20.film, q

9.3 See the end of these answers

9.4 See the end of these answers

9.5 **Across** 1.angry 3.thirsty 5.nice 6.dangerous 8.dark 9.beautiful 11.possible 13.fair 15.Happy 16.dirty 17.interested 20.extra 21.free 22.big 23.quiet 24.difficult   **Down** 1.afraid 2.good 3.terrible 4.useful 7.different 10.untidy 12.important 14.icy 15.hot 18.tired 19.right

9.6 **Across** 1.around 4.something 8.like 9.my 10.down 12.she 14.at 16.so 18.house 21.mean 22.those 24.year 25.do 26.yes 28.course 29.without 34.still 36.up 37.for 38.last 40.old 41.take 42.really 43.another   **Down** 1.against 2.only 3.does 4.same 5.end 6.How 7.got 11.other 13.as 15.the 16.says 17.one 19.under 20.to 21.May 23.such 27.people 28.children 29.world 30.this 31.off 32.through 33.used 35.little 39.than

9.7 2.talk 3.tall 4.wall 5.fall 6.fill 7.will 8.hill 9.hall 10.half 11.Halt 12.salt 13.sale 14.male

Test 1 1.d 2.b 3.d 4.a 5.a 6.b 7.b 8.d 9.c 10.d 11.d 12.b 13.a 14.d 15.a

Test 2 1.c 2.d 3.c 4.d 5.d 6.d 7.d 8.c 9.b 10.d 11.b 12.a 13.a 14.d 15.a

Test 3 1.d 2.b 3.a 4.c 5.d 6.c 7.b 8.a 9.b 10.b 11.d 12.b 13.d 14.a 15.c

Test 4 1.b 2.d 3.b 4.c 5.d 6.d 7.d 8.a 9.b 10.a 11.c 12.c 13.c 14.d 15.d

Test 5 1.a 2.c 3.a 4.c 5.b 6.c 7.b 8.b 9.d 10.b 11.d 12.a 13.b 14.d 15.b

9.3 Puzzle Solution   9.4 Puzzle Solution

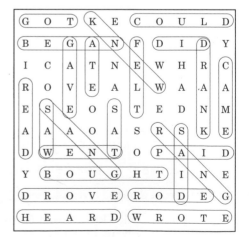